Ultimate Guide to Franchise Marketing

Author: Harry Gallimore-King
Edition: New edition
Copyright Year: 2024
Copyright Holder: Harry Gallimore-King

ISBN: 978-1-304-12190-5

Published by:
Imprint: Lulu.com

First and foremost, I would like to express my deepest gratitude to my husband, Nathan. Your unwavering support, encouragement, and belief in me have been the foundation of all that I do. From the long days to the late nights, your understanding and love have kept me grounded and motivated.

I would also like to extend my heartfelt thanks to the entire team at Growth Alliance. Your dedication and commitment to excellence have been an inspiration to me. It is because of our collective efforts that this book has been made possible. A special mention to the leadership at Growth Alliance for trusting me with the responsibility of heading operations and allowing me the creative freedom to explore and implement strategies that have contributed to the success of our clients.

Lastly, I would like to thank all the franchisees and franchisors I have had the pleasure of working with over the years. Your drive to succeed and willingness to embrace new ideas have been the true inspiration behind this book. It is my hope that the strategies, tips, and insights shared here will empower you to take your marketing efforts to the next level.

In today's rapidly evolving digital landscape, the importance of a well-coordinated and unified marketing strategy cannot be overstated—especially for franchisees and franchisors. The tools at our disposal, such as Google Ads, Google Business Profiles, Facebook Ads, and Instagram Ads, offer unparalleled opportunities to reach and engage with potential customers. However, the sheer volume of options and the technical nature of these platforms can be overwhelming, particularly for those who are new to digital marketing.

This book is designed to bridge that gap. Drawing on my extensive experience working with a diverse range of clients across various markets, I have crafted this guide to be both accessible and actionable. Whether you're a franchisee looking to boost local visibility or a franchisor aiming to support your network with cohesive marketing strategies, this book will provide you with the knowledge and tools you need to succeed.

Throughout the chapters, you will find a blend of strategic advice, practical tips, and real-life examples drawn from my career. These examples are not just theoretical—they are proven approaches that have delivered tangible results for businesses like yours. In addition, I've included activities designed to help you apply what you've learned and see the impact of your efforts firsthand.

The central theme of this book is the power of a unified approach. By integrating your efforts across different platforms, you can create a marketing machine that is greater than the sum of its parts. But I also recognize that every business is unique, and there is no one-size-fits-all solution. That's why I've also explored alternative approaches, allowing you to tailor your strategy to fit your specific needs and goals.

I hope this book serves as a valuable resource as you navigate the complex world of digital marketing. Remember, the journey to mastering these tools is a marathon, not a sprint. Take it one step at a time, and soon you'll find that what once seemed daunting has become second nature.

Contents

Chapter 1: Introduction to Digital Marketing for Franchisees and Franchisors

Understanding the Digital Landscape

The digital landscape has dramatically transformed the way businesses operate over the past two decades. The rise of the internet and the proliferation of smartphones have given consumers unprecedented access to information, products, and services. As a result, the traditional methods of marketing, which once relied heavily on print media, television, and radio, have been supplemented—and in many cases, supplanted—by digital marketing strategies.

For franchisees and franchisors, this digital transformation presents both opportunities and challenges. On one hand, digital marketing tools such as Google Ads, Google Business Profiles, Facebook Ads, and Instagram Ads offer the ability to reach a broader audience with greater precision and at a lower cost compared to traditional media. On the other hand, the sheer number of options and the technical complexity of these tools can be overwhelming, especially for those new to digital marketing.

In the simplest terms, digital marketing refers to any marketing efforts that use an electronic device or the internet. Businesses leverage digital channels such as search engines, social media, email, and websites to connect with current and prospective customers. Understanding these channels and how they interact with one another is crucial for any successful marketing strategy, particularly in the context of franchising, where the brand identity must be maintained across multiple locations while allowing for local adaptation.

The Evolution of Digital Marketing

To fully grasp the significance of digital marketing, it's important to understand how it has evolved over the years. In the early days of the internet, digital marketing primarily consisted of banner ads and email marketing. These were relatively straightforward methods of reaching customers but lacked the sophistication and targeting capabilities that we see today.

As search engines like Google became the primary gateway to the internet, search engine marketing (SEM) and search engine optimisation (SEO) emerged as critical components of digital marketing. Businesses began to realise that appearing at the top of search results could dramatically increase visibility and drive more traffic to their websites. This led to the development of pay-per-click (PPC) advertising models, where businesses could bid on keywords to have their ads displayed alongside search results.

The advent of social media platforms like Facebook, Twitter, and Instagram marked the next major evolution in digital marketing. These platforms provided businesses with new ways to engage with their audience, build brand loyalty, and drive sales. Social media advertising, which allows for highly targeted campaigns based on user demographics, interests, and behaviours, has become a cornerstone of modern digital marketing strategies.

More recently, the rise of mobile devices has further transformed the digital landscape. With more people accessing the internet via smartphones than desktop computers, businesses must now ensure that their digital marketing efforts are mobile-friendly. This includes everything from responsive website design to mobile-specific ad formats.

Why Digital Marketing is Essential for Franchises

For franchise businesses, digital marketing is not just an option—it's a necessity. In today's competitive market, customers expect to find the information they need online, whether they're looking for a product, a service, or simply trying to find the nearest location of a brand they trust. If your franchise isn't visible in the digital space, you're missing out on a significant portion of potential customers.

Digital marketing also allows for a level of targeting and personalisation that was previously impossible. With tools like Google Ads and Facebook Ads, you can tailor your marketing messages to specific demographics, geographic areas, and even individual customer preferences. This is particularly valuable for franchises, where different locations may serve different types of customers.

Moreover, digital marketing provides measurable results. Unlike traditional marketing methods, where it can be difficult to gauge the effectiveness of a campaign, digital marketing allows you to track metrics like website traffic, conversion rates, and return on investment (ROI). This data-driven approach enables you to continuously refine and optimise your marketing efforts, ensuring that you're getting the best possible results.

The Importance of a Unified Marketing Strategy

One of the most critical concepts in digital marketing for franchises is the idea of a unified marketing strategy. While each digital platform has its unique features and strengths, the real power of digital marketing lies in the synergy that can be achieved when these platforms are used together in a coordinated manner.

The Dangers of a Fragmented Approach

Too often, businesses—especially those operating within a franchise model—fall into the trap of treating each marketing channel as a separate entity. For example, a franchisee might focus solely on running Google Ads to drive local traffic, while the franchisor is more concerned with maintaining a strong social media presence. While these efforts may yield some results on their own, they can lead to a fragmented and inconsistent brand experience.

A fragmented approach can create several problems. First, it can lead to mixed messaging, where customers receive conflicting information depending on which channel they encounter. For instance, a customer might see a promotion on Facebook that isn't reflected in the Google Ads they encounter later. This inconsistency can erode trust and confuse potential customers.

Second, a fragmented approach often results in inefficiencies. Without a coordinated strategy, different parts of the business may end up duplicating efforts or competing for the same audience. This can lead to wasted resources and missed opportunities.

The Power of a Unified Strategy

In contrast, a unified marketing strategy ensures that all your marketing efforts are aligned with your brand's goals and messaging, creating a seamless experience for your audience. This approach not only maximises the impact of each campaign but also helps in building a stronger, more recognisable brand presence across all platforms.

A unified strategy involves several key components:

1. **Consistent Messaging:** All marketing materials, whether they're on Google Ads, Facebook, Instagram, or your website, should convey the

same core messages. This ensures that customers receive a cohesive experience, regardless of how they interact with your brand.

2. **Integrated Campaigns:** Rather than running separate campaigns on different platforms, consider how they can work together. For example, you might use Google Ads to drive traffic to a landing page, which then encourages visitors to follow your business on Facebook or Instagram for exclusive offers.

3. **Shared Data and Insights:** One of the biggest advantages of digital marketing is the ability to collect and analyse data. By sharing insights across different platforms, you can make more informed decisions and continuously improve your strategy. For instance, if a particular demographic responds well to your Facebook Ads, you might consider targeting them more heavily in your Google Ads campaigns as well.

4. **Collaboration Between Franchisees and Franchisors:** In a franchise model, it's essential that franchisees and franchisors work together to create a unified marketing strategy. Franchisees should have access to the resources and support they need to execute local campaigns that align with the overall brand strategy. Meanwhile, franchisors should provide clear guidelines and tools to ensure consistency across all locations.

Consider this analogy: imagine your marketing efforts as a symphony orchestra. Each instrument represents a different platform—Google Ads, Google Business Profiles, Facebook Ads, and Instagram Ads. On their own, these instruments can create music, but when they are all playing in harmony, led by a conductor with a clear vision (your unified strategy), they can create a masterpiece.

Real-World Example: A Unified Strategy in Action

To illustrate the power of a unified strategy, let's look at a real-world example. Imagine a nationwide coffee shop franchise that wants to increase foot traffic and brand loyalty. The franchisor develops a national campaign centred around the launch of a new seasonal beverage. This campaign includes:

- **Google Ads** targeting keywords related to seasonal drinks and coffee shops, driving traffic to a dedicated landing page where customers can find their nearest location.
- **Facebook Ads** featuring videos and images of the new beverage, with a call-to-action to visit the nearest shop and try it.
- **Instagram Ads** using influencer marketing to create buzz around the launch, with influencers sharing their experiences trying the new drink.

At the same time, each franchisee is encouraged to run local campaigns that align with the national strategy. They might:

- **Use Google Business Profiles** to update their location's information with details about the new drink, including photos and posts promoting it.
- **Run local Facebook and Instagram Ads** targeting people within a certain radius of their shop, offering a special discount to those who mention the ad when they visit.

By coordinating their efforts across multiple platforms and locations, the franchise creates a powerful and cohesive campaign that drives results at both the national and local levels.

Key Platforms: Google Ads, Google Business Profiles, Facebook Ads, and Instagram Ads

Now that we've established the importance of a unified marketing strategy, let's take a closer look at the key digital marketing platforms that will be the focus of this book. Each platform has its strengths and is best suited for different aspects of your marketing strategy. Understanding these nuances will help you decide how to allocate your resources effectively.

Google Ads

Google Ads is one of the most powerful tools available to businesses today. It allows you to create highly targeted campaigns that appear in search results, on YouTube, or across Google's Display Network. For franchisees and franchisors, Google Ads can be particularly effective for driving local traffic, promoting special offers, and increasing brand visibility.

Google Ads operates on a pay-per-click (PPC) model, meaning you only pay when someone clicks on your ad. This makes it a cost-effective option, especially for businesses with limited marketing budgets. However, the key to success with Google Ads lies in understanding your audience and using the platform's targeting options to reach them effectively.

Google Business Profiles

Formerly known as Google My Business, Google Business Profiles are essential for any business with a physical location. For franchisees, maintaining an up-to-date and optimised Google Business Profile is crucial for local SEO (Search Engine Optimisation) and for appearing in local search results. It's often the first interaction a potential customer will have with your business, so making a strong impression is vital.

Google Business Profiles allow you to manage how your business appears in Google Search and Maps. By ensuring that your profile is complete, accurate, and engaging, you can increase your chances of attracting local customers. Features such as reviews, photos, and posts can also enhance your profile and encourage customer interaction.

Facebook Ads

Facebook remains one of the most widely used social media platforms, making it an invaluable tool for reaching a broad and diverse audience. Facebook Ads offer detailed targeting options, allowing you to reach specific demographics based on age, location, interests, and behaviours.

For franchisees and franchisors, Facebook Ads can be particularly effective for brand awareness campaigns, promoting events, and engaging with the local community. The platform's ad formats, which include carousel ads, video ads, and lead generation forms, provide flexibility in how you present your message to your audience.

Instagram Ads

Instagram, owned by Facebook, is a visual-centric platform that is ideal for brands looking to engage with audiences through images and short videos. For franchisees, Instagram Ads offer an opportunity to showcase products, services, and customer experiences in a visually appealing way.

Instagram's ad formats, such as Stories ads and Explore ads, allow businesses to reach users in creative and immersive ways. The platform is particularly popular among younger demographics, making it a key player in any digital marketing strategy aimed at millennials and Gen Z.

Case Study: The Power of Integration

Consider the case of a franchise in the fitness industry, where the franchisor and franchisees work together on a unified digital marketing strategy. The franchisor launches a campaign to promote a new fitness challenge, which is advertised through:

- **Google Ads:** Targeting keywords related to fitness challenges, weight loss, and gym memberships.
- **Facebook Ads:** Featuring testimonials and success stories from participants in previous challenges, with a link to sign up.
- **Instagram Ads:** Using influencers in the fitness industry to create buzz around the challenge, sharing their own experiences and encouraging their followers to join.

At the local level, each franchisee supports the campaign by:

- **Optimising their Google Business Profile** to highlight the fitness challenge, including new photos, posts, and customer reviews.
- **Running local Facebook and Instagram Ads** targeting people in their area who are interested in fitness and wellness, offering a discount for early sign-ups.

The result is a highly effective campaign that leverages the strengths of each platform while maintaining a consistent message across all channels. The integration of efforts at the national and local levels ensures that the franchise maximises its reach and impact, ultimately driving more sign-ups and increasing brand loyalty.

Why This Book?

You might be wondering why a book specifically for franchisees and franchisors is necessary. The answer lies in the unique challenges and opportunities that the franchise model presents. Unlike standalone businesses, franchises must balance the need for a cohesive brand identity with the autonomy of individual franchisees. This balancing act can make digital marketing more complex, but also more rewarding when done correctly.

Franchisees often face the challenge of standing out in a crowded market while adhering to the brand guidelines set by the franchisor. On the other hand, franchisors need to support their network of franchisees with marketing strategies that are scalable, effective, and adaptable to different markets.

This book is designed to address these specific challenges. It will provide you with actionable strategies, real-life examples, and practical tips that you can implement in your own business. Whether you're a franchisee looking to boost your local presence or a franchisor aiming to create a unified marketing strategy across your network, this book will serve as a valuable resource.

Activity: Assess Your Current Digital Presence

Before we dive deeper into each platform, it's important to take stock of your current digital presence. This activity will help you identify areas of strength and opportunities for improvement.

1. **Google Yourself:** Start by searching for your business on Google. Take note of where your business appears in the search results. Is your Google Business Profile visible? Are there any other mentions of your business? This will give you an initial idea of your visibility on Google.

2. **Review Your Google Business Profile:** If you have a Google Business Profile, review the information it contains. Is it accurate and up to date? Are there any areas that could be improved, such as adding more photos or responding to reviews?
3. **Check Your Social Media Profiles:** Visit your business's Facebook and Instagram profiles. Are they consistent with your brand's identity? Do they engage with your audience? Make a note of any improvements that could be made.
4. **Analyse Your Ad Campaigns:** If you're already running Google Ads, Facebook Ads, or Instagram Ads, take some time to review their performance. Are they delivering the results you expected? Are there opportunities to optimise your campaigns?
5. **Competitor Analysis:** Take a look at your competitors' digital presence. How do they appear in search results? What are they doing on social media? Are there any strategies they're using that you could adapt for your own business?
6. **Customer Feedback:** Reach out to a few of your loyal customers and ask them about their experience finding your business online. Were there any challenges they faced? What did they like or dislike about your digital presence? Use this feedback to guide your improvements.

By completing this activity, you'll have a clearer picture of your current digital presence and be better prepared to implement the strategies discussed in the following chapters.

Looking Ahead

Now that you have a basic understanding of the digital landscape and the importance of a unified marketing strategy, we're ready to dive deeper into each platform. In the next chapter, we'll start by laying the foundation for your digital presence, beginning with Google Business Profiles and setting up your social media accounts. This will set the stage for more advanced strategies and ensure that you have a solid foundation to build on.

Remember, digital marketing is not about quick fixes; it's about building a sustainable strategy that will deliver long-term results. With the right approach, the tools and platforms at your disposal can become powerful allies in your journey towards business growth and success.

Chapter 2: Laying the Foundation: Setting Up Your Digital Presence

Introduction

Before diving into the intricacies of digital advertising, it is essential to establish a robust foundation for your online presence. Whether you're a franchisee aiming to dominate your local market or a franchisor seeking consistency across multiple locations, the first step is ensuring that your business is easily discoverable and well-represented online. This chapter will guide you through the process of setting up and optimising your Google Business Profile, as well as creating a cohesive presence on social media platforms like Facebook and Instagram.

A well-established digital presence not only enhances your visibility but also builds credibility with potential customers. In the digital age, a business that is difficult to find online might as well not exist. Customers expect to find information quickly and easily, and they are more likely to choose a business that has a strong and positive online presence.

In this chapter, we'll explore the essential steps to setting up your digital presence, ensuring that your business stands out in local search results, engages effectively with customers, and leverages the power of social media to build a loyal community around your brand.

Google Business Profiles: Your Digital Front Door

For many potential customers, your Google Business Profile (GBP) will be their first interaction with your brand. It appears when someone searches for your business or related services on Google Search or Maps, making it a crucial tool for local search engine optimisation (SEO). A well-optimised GBP can significantly increase your visibility, drive more traffic to your website or physical location, and enhance your credibility.

Setting Up Your Google Business Profile

1. **Creating Your Profile:**
   - Visit Google Business Profile and sign in with your Google account. If your business is already listed, you can claim it by searching for your business name. If it's not listed, you can create a new profile by providing your business name, address, and contact details.
   - Verify your business through one of Google's verification methods, such as receiving a postcard at your business address or verifying by phone or email. Verification is crucial as it ensures that your business information is accurate and gives you control over the profile.
2. **Completing Your Profile:**
   - Ensure that all essential information is filled out, including your business name, address, phone number, and website. Consistency is key, so make sure that these details match the information on your website and other online directories.
   - Choose the most accurate and specific business category. This helps Google understand what your business offers and improves your chances of appearing in relevant searches.
   - Add your business hours, including any special hours for holidays or events. Keeping this information up to date is important to avoid disappointing potential customers.
3. **Enhancing Your Profile:**
   - Upload high-quality photos of your business, products, and services. Profiles

with photos receive more clicks and engagement, so invest time in selecting images that showcase your brand in the best light.

- o Encourage customers to leave reviews on your GBP. Positive reviews build trust and can influence potential customers' decisions. Responding to reviews—both positive and negative—demonstrates your commitment to customer service.
- o Use the "Posts" feature to share updates, offers, and events directly on your GBP. Regularly posting content keeps your profile active and provides more reasons for customers to engage with your business.

4. **Advanced Optimisation Techniques:**
   - o **Utilise Keywords:** Incorporate relevant keywords in your business description and posts. This improves your profile's visibility in search results.
   - o **Add a Virtual Tour:** If possible, add a virtual tour of your business premises. This feature can make your profile more engaging and give customers a better sense of what to expect when they visit.
   - o **Monitor Insights:** Google provides valuable insights into how customers are interacting with your profile, such as how they found your business and what actions they took. Use this data to refine your profile and marketing strategies.

Managing Multiple Locations

If you're a franchisor or a franchisee managing multiple locations, maintaining consistency across all profiles is vital. Google offers tools such as bulk location management, which allows you to update information across multiple profiles simultaneously. Ensuring that each location's profile is optimised and regularly updated will help maintain a strong brand presence across different markets.

Managing multiple locations also involves localising content where appropriate. While consistency is important, it's also beneficial to tailor certain aspects of your profile to reflect the unique characteristics of each location. For instance, the photos you use might differ to showcase the distinct environment of each location, or the posts you share could highlight local events or promotions.

Case Study: The Impact of an Optimised Google Business Profile

Consider a franchisee of a popular restaurant chain who diligently optimises their Google Business Profile. By ensuring that all information is accurate, uploading appealing photos of the restaurant and its dishes, and regularly posting updates about new menu items and promotions, the franchisee sees a significant increase in local search traffic.

Within three months, the restaurant's GBP views double, and customer calls for reservations increase by 40%. Additionally, the number of customers who find the restaurant via Google Maps and decide to visit on the spot also grows, leading to a noticeable uptick in walk-in traffic. This case study illustrates how a well-maintained GBP can directly contribute to business growth.

Establishing a Strong Social Media Presence

Once your Google Business Profile is set up, the next step is to establish a cohesive presence on social media platforms, specifically Facebook and Instagram. Social media is not just about promoting your business; it's about building a community and engaging with your audience on a more personal level.

A strong social media presence can increase brand awareness, drive traffic to your website, and create opportunities for direct engagement with your customers. In today's digital world, consumers expect brands to be active on social media, and they often turn to these platforms for customer service, reviews, and the latest news and updates.

Setting Up Your Facebook Business Page

1. **Creating Your Page:**
   - Go to Facebook Business and click on "Create a Page." Select the appropriate category for your business, such as "Local Business" or "Brand," and enter your business name and details.
   - Add a profile picture and cover photo that represent your brand. These images should be high-quality and consistent with your branding across other platforms.
   - Fill out your business information, including contact details, hours of operation, and a short description. Like with your Google Business Profile, consistency is important.
2. **Customising Your Page:**
   - Add a call-to-action (CTA) button to your page, such as "Call Now" or "Book Appointment." This makes it easier for visitors to take the next step towards engaging with your business.
   - Create and organise tabs on your page, such as "Services," "Shop," or "Reviews," depending on what is most relevant to your business. Custom tabs help visitors

navigate your page more easily and find the information they're looking for.

3. **Engaging with Your Audience:**
   - Post regular content that resonates with your audience. This could include promotions, customer testimonials, behind-the-scenes glimpses, or industry-related news. The goal is to keep your audience engaged and coming back for more.
   - Respond to comments and messages promptly. Social media is a two-way street, and engaging with your audience helps build trust and loyalty.

4. **Leveraging Facebook Insights:**
   - Facebook provides detailed analytics through Facebook Insights. Use these insights to understand your audience better, track the performance of your posts, and refine your content strategy. Pay attention to metrics like reach, engagement, and conversions to determine what types of content are most effective.

Setting Up Your Instagram Business Account

1. **Converting to a Business Account:**
   - If you already have a personal Instagram account, you can convert it to a business account by going to your profile settings and selecting "Switch to Professional Account." If you're starting from scratch, you can create a new account directly as a business account.
   - Link your Instagram account to your Facebook Page. This integration allows you to manage both platforms more efficiently and run ads across both with ease.

2. **Optimising Your Profile:**
   - Choose a profile picture that matches your Facebook Page's profile picture to maintain consistency. This is often your logo or another recognisable brand image.
   - Write a concise and compelling bio that describes your business and includes a call-to-action, such as a link to your website or a special offer.
   - Add contact options to your profile, such as an email address or phone number, to make it easy for followers to reach you directly.
3. **Creating a Content Strategy:**
   - Instagram is a visual platform, so focus on creating high-quality images and videos that tell your brand's story. This could include product showcases, customer experiences, or behind-the-scenes content.
   - Use hashtags strategically to increase your reach. Research popular and relevant hashtags in your industry and incorporate them into your posts.
   - Engage with your audience by liking, commenting on, and sharing user-generated content. Building a community around your brand on Instagram can lead to higher engagement and loyalty.
4. **Utilising Instagram Stories and IGTV:**
   - Instagram Stories allow you to share short, engaging content that disappears after 24 hours. Use Stories to share timely updates, special promotions, or behind-the-scenes glimpses of your business. Since Stories are more ephemeral, they offer a great way to experiment with content and engage your audience in a more informal, immediate way.

- IGTV (Instagram TV) allows you to post longer videos, which can be useful for more in-depth content such as tutorials, interviews, or event coverage. By regularly posting on IGTV, you can provide value to your followers and position your brand as an authority in your industry.

The Role of Consistency Across Platforms

As you set up your digital presence across Google, Facebook, and Instagram, it's important to maintain consistency in your branding. This includes using the same logos, colour schemes, and messaging across all platforms. Consistency not only helps in building a strong brand identity but also ensures that customers recognise your business regardless of where they encounter it online.

Consistency also extends to how you interact with your audience. Whether responding to a review on Google, replying to a comment on Facebook, or liking a post on Instagram, your tone and approach should reflect your brand's personality and values. Consistent communication helps build trust with your audience, making them more likely to engage with your brand and become loyal customers.

Case Study: The Power of Consistent Branding

A local bakery franchise decided to revamp its digital presence by ensuring consistent branding across all platforms. They updated their Google Business Profile with new photos and a detailed description, synchronised their Facebook and Instagram profiles with the same images and bio, and began posting regularly across all channels with a unified voice.

The results were immediate and impactful. Within two months, the bakery saw a 25% increase in followers on Instagram, a 30% increase in engagement on Facebook, and a significant uptick in online orders through their website. Customers began mentioning the brand's new social media presence in their reviews, praising the engaging content and consistent communication.

This case study illustrates the importance of maintaining a cohesive brand identity across all digital platforms. By presenting a unified front, the bakery was able to strengthen its relationship with existing customers while attracting new ones.

Activity: Establishing and Optimising Your Digital Profiles

Now that you've learned the basics of setting up your digital presence, it's time to put that knowledge into action. This activity will guide you through the process of creating or optimising your Google Business Profile, Facebook Page, and Instagram account.

1. **Create or Claim Your Google Business Profile:**
   o If you haven't already done so, create or claim your Google Business Profile. Complete all sections of the profile, ensuring that the information is accurate and up-to-date. Don't forget to verify your business.
2. **Set Up Your Facebook Page:**
   o If you don't have a Facebook Page for your business, create one now. If you already have a page, review it to ensure that all information is accurate and consistent with your other online profiles.
3. **Create or Convert Your Instagram Account:**
   o If you're not already on Instagram, set up a business account. If you have a personal

account that you'd like to use for your business, convert it to a professional account and optimise your profile.

4. **Review and Align Branding Across Platforms:**
   - Take some time to review your profiles on all platforms. Are the logos, colours, and messaging consistent? Make any necessary adjustments to ensure a cohesive brand presence.

5. **Post an Introductory Update:**
   - On each platform, post an introductory update or status that welcomes visitors to your page or profile. This could be a brief message about your business, what you offer, and what followers can expect to see in the future.

6. **Engage with Your Audience:**
   - Start engaging with your audience by responding to comments, liking posts, and sharing user-generated content. The more you interact, the more likely you are to build a loyal community.

7. **Track Your Progress:**
   - Use the analytics tools provided by Google, Facebook, and Instagram to monitor your progress. Pay attention to key metrics such as views, clicks, likes, shares, and conversions. Use this data to refine your strategy and make informed decisions about your digital marketing efforts.

By completing this activity, you will have established a solid foundation for your digital marketing efforts. With your profiles set up and optimised, you're now ready to explore the more advanced strategies that will drive traffic, engagement, and sales.

Looking Ahead

With your digital presence firmly in place, the next step is to dive into the world of advertising. In the following chapters, we'll explore how to create and manage effective ad campaigns on Google, Facebook, and Instagram. You'll learn how to target the right audience, craft compelling ads, and measure the success of your campaigns.

Remember, the foundation you've just built is crucial. A strong, well-maintained digital presence will enhance the effectiveness of your advertising efforts and ensure that you're making the most of your marketing budget. As you move forward, keep your profiles updated and continue engaging with your audience regularly. This ongoing effort will pay dividends as you grow your brand and reach more customers.

Chapter 3: Crafting a Unified Marketing Strategy

Introduction

With a solid digital presence established, the next critical step in your digital marketing journey is crafting a unified marketing strategy. This chapter will guide you through the process of integrating your efforts across different platforms—Google Ads, Google Business Profiles, Facebook Ads, and Instagram Ads—to create a cohesive and effective marketing campaign. We will also explore how to align franchisee and franchisor marketing goals, ensuring consistency while allowing for local flexibility.

A unified marketing strategy is not just about running ads on different platforms; it's about creating a seamless experience for your customers. Whether they find your business through a Google search, a Facebook post, or an Instagram ad, the messaging, branding, and call-to-action should be consistent and reinforce each other. This chapter will show you how to achieve that consistency and why it's so important for the success of your franchise.

The Components of a Unified Marketing Strategy

A unified marketing strategy consists of several key components, each of which plays a vital role in creating a cohesive and effective campaign. These components include:

1. **Brand Consistency:**
   - **Visual Identity:** Your brand's visual identity—logos, colours, fonts, and imagery—should be consistent across all platforms. This ensures that customers immediately recognise your brand, regardless of where they encounter it.

- o **Messaging:** Your brand's voice, tone, and key messages should also be consistent. Whether you're writing a Google ad, a Facebook post, or an Instagram caption, the language should reflect your brand's personality and values.
- o **Customer Experience:** The experience you provide to customers, both online and offline, should be seamless and aligned with your brand's promises. This includes everything from the ease of navigating your website to the quality of service in your physical locations.

2. **Integrated Campaigns:**
   - o **Cross-Platform Strategies:** Rather than viewing each platform in isolation, consider how they can work together to amplify your message. For example, you might run a Google Ads campaign to drive traffic to your website, where visitors can sign up for a newsletter that you promote on Facebook and Instagram.
   - o **Sequential Advertising:** This involves using multiple touchpoints to guide potential customers through the buyer's journey. For instance, you could start with a broad awareness campaign on Instagram, followed by a more targeted Google Ads campaign for users who visited your site but didn't make a purchase, and finally a Facebook remarketing ad offering a discount to those who still haven't converted.

3. **Data-Driven Decision Making:**
   - o **Analytics and Reporting:** Use the analytics tools provided by each platform to track the performance of your campaigns. Look at metrics such as click-through rates (CTR), conversion rates, and

return on ad spend (ROAS) to assess what's working and what isn't.

- ○ **A/B Testing:** Experiment with different versions of your ads, landing pages, and calls-to-action to see which performs best. A/B testing allows you to make data-driven decisions and optimise your campaigns for better results.
- ○ **Customer Feedback:** Incorporate feedback from your customers to refine your strategy. This could come from reviews, social media comments, or direct customer surveys.

4. **Collaboration Between Franchisees and Franchisors:**
   - ○ **Guidelines and Support:** Franchisors should provide clear guidelines on brand usage, messaging, and marketing strategies while offering support and resources to franchisees. This ensures that all marketing efforts are aligned with the overall brand strategy.
   - ○ **Local Flexibility:** Franchisees should be empowered to tailor their marketing efforts to their local market. This could involve adjusting the messaging to reflect local culture, promoting location-specific events or offers, or focusing on platforms that are particularly popular in their area.
   - ○ **Shared Goals:** Both franchisees and franchisors should work towards shared marketing goals, such as increasing brand awareness, driving traffic to physical locations, or boosting online sales. Regular communication and collaboration are key to achieving these goals.

Building a Cohesive Brand Identity

At the heart of a unified marketing strategy is a strong, cohesive brand identity. Your brand identity is what sets you apart from your competitors and what customers will come to recognise and trust. A cohesive brand identity not only makes your marketing more effective but also builds brand loyalty, which is crucial for long-term success.

Defining Your Brand

Before you can create a cohesive brand identity, you need to clearly define what your brand stands for. This includes:

1. **Brand Values:** What are the core values that your brand represents? These might include things like quality, innovation, customer service, or sustainability. Your brand values should be reflected in everything you do; from the products you offer to the way you interact with customers.
2. **Brand Personality:** How would you describe your brand's personality? Is it friendly and approachable, or more professional and authoritative? Your brand's personality should be evident in your messaging, visual identity, and customer interactions.
3. **Unique Selling Proposition (USP):** What sets your brand apart from the competition? Your USP is the unique benefit or advantage that your brand offers to customers. It should be the central message of your marketing campaigns and consistently communicated across all platforms.

Consistency Across All Platforms

Once you've defined your brand, the next step is to ensure that it is consistently represented across all marketing platforms. This involves:

1. **Visual Branding:** Your logo, colour scheme, fonts, and imagery should be the same across all platforms. This not only helps with brand recognition but also creates a professional and polished look for your business. Ensure that all franchisees have access to high-quality versions of your brand assets and understand how to use them correctly.
2. **Messaging:** Your brand's key messages—such as your USP, brand values, and any taglines or slogans—should be used consistently across all platforms. This doesn't mean that every piece of content needs to be identical, but the core message should always be clear and aligned with your brand identity.
3. **Customer Interactions:** Whether a customer is interacting with your brand on social media, through email, or in person at one of your locations, the experience should feel consistent. This includes the tone of voice used in communications, the level of customer service provided, and the overall customer journey.

Case Study: Consistency in Action

Let's look at a case study of a successful franchise that excels in maintaining a cohesive brand identity across multiple platforms. Consider a global fitness franchise that has built a strong brand around the concept of community and empowerment.

- **Visual Identity:** The franchise uses the same vibrant colour scheme, bold fonts, and energetic imagery across all platforms. Whether you visit their website, follow them on Instagram, or walk into one of their gyms, the visual experience is consistent and instantly recognisable.
- **Messaging:** The franchise's messaging focuses on inclusivity, motivation, and results. This

messaging is consistently communicated across all platforms, from motivational posts on Facebook to success stories shared on their website. Every piece of content reinforces the brand's core message: that everyone is welcome, and everyone can achieve their fitness goals with the right support.

- **Customer Experience:** The experience of joining a class at one of their gyms mirrors the experience of interacting with the brand online. Instructors are trained to deliver the same motivational messages that are used in the franchise's marketing, creating a seamless experience for customers.

The result of this consistency is a strong, loyal customer base that feels connected to the brand, whether they're engaging with it online or in person.

Aligning Franchisee and Franchisor Marketing Goals

One of the unique challenges of franchise marketing is aligning the goals of franchisees with those of the franchisor. While the franchisor is focused on maintaining a strong, consistent brand identity and expanding the franchise network, franchisees are more concerned with driving traffic to their specific location and meeting local sales targets. A successful unified marketing strategy needs to balance these goals.

Setting Shared Goals

The first step in aligning franchisee and franchisor marketing goals is to establish shared objectives that benefit both parties. These might include:

1. **Brand Awareness:** Increasing brand awareness is a goal that benefits both franchisors and franchisees. By boosting recognition of the brand

on a national or even global scale, franchisors create a stronger market presence that all franchisees can benefit from.

2. **Customer Acquisition:** Both franchisors and franchisees have a vested interest in acquiring new customers. While the franchisor may focus on broader campaigns that drive brand awareness and lead generation, franchisees can focus on local marketing efforts that convert leads into paying customers.

3. **Customer Retention:** Retaining existing customers is often more cost-effective than acquiring new ones, and it's a goal that benefits both franchisors and franchisees. Loyalty programs, email marketing, and exceptional customer service are all strategies that can help increase customer retention.

4. **Sales Growth:** Ultimately, the success of both the franchisor and the franchisee depends on increasing sales. By working together to create effective marketing campaigns, both parties can achieve their sales targets and contribute to the overall growth of the franchise.

Supporting Franchisee Autonomy

While it's important to have shared goals, it's also crucial to recognise that each franchisee operates in a unique market with its own challenges and opportunities. As such, franchisees need a certain level of autonomy to tailor their marketing efforts to their local audience.

- **Localised Content:** Encourage franchisees to create content that is relevant to their local market. This might include highlighting local events, featuring local customers in testimonials, or running promotions that appeal to the local community. While the core messaging should remain consistent with the overall brand, localised content can help franchisees connect with their audience on a more personal level.

- **Flexible Campaigns:** Provide franchisees with flexible marketing templates that they can adapt to their needs. For example, you might provide a standard ad template that franchisees can customise with their location's details and specific offers. This allows franchisees to maintain brand consistency while also addressing the needs of their local market.
- **Training and Resources:** Offer training and resources to help franchisees develop their marketing skills and implement effective campaigns. This might include workshops on social media marketing, guides on creating effective Google Ads, or one-on-one support from the franchisor's marketing team.

Regular Communication and Collaboration

To ensure that both franchisees and franchisors are working towards the same goals, regular communication and collaboration are essential. This might involve:

1. **Monthly Marketing Meetings:** Hold monthly marketing meetings where franchisees can share their successes and challenges, and the franchisor can provide updates on upcoming campaigns and brand initiatives.
2. **Marketing Portals:** Create an online marketing portal where franchisees can access resources, templates, and brand guidelines. This ensures that all franchisees have the tools they need to execute effective marketing campaigns.
3. **Feedback Loops:** Establish feedback loops where franchisees can share insights from their local market, and the franchisor can use this information to refine the overall marketing strategy. This two-way communication helps

ensure that the marketing strategy is effective at both the national and local levels.

Activity: Developing Your Unified Marketing Strategy

Now that you understand the components of a unified marketing strategy, it's time to start developing your own. This activity will guide you through the process of creating a strategy that aligns with your brand's goals and allows for local flexibility.

1. **Define Your Brand Identity:**
   - Write down your brand's core values, personality, and unique selling proposition. Ensure that all stakeholders, including franchisees, have a clear understanding of what your brand stands for.
2. **Set Shared Marketing Goals:**
   - Identify the key marketing goals that will benefit both the franchisor and franchisees. These might include increasing brand awareness, acquiring new customers, or boosting sales.
3. **Create a Visual Branding Guide:**
   - Develop a visual branding guide that outlines how your logo, colours, fonts, and imagery should be used across all platforms. Share this guide with all franchisees to ensure consistency.
4. **Develop Cross-Platform Campaigns:**
   - Plan a marketing campaign that integrates multiple platforms, such as Google Ads, Facebook Ads, and Instagram Ads. Ensure that the messaging, visual identity, and call-to-action are consistent across all channels.
5. **Encourage Localisation:**
   - Create templates and resources that allow franchisees to localise their marketing

efforts. Provide guidance on how to maintain brand consistency while tailoring content to the local market.

6. **Establish Communication Channels:**
   - Set up regular communication channels, such as monthly marketing meetings or an online portal, to facilitate collaboration between the franchisor and franchisees.

7. **Monitor and Refine:**
   - Use analytics tools to monitor the performance of your marketing campaigns. Collect feedback from franchisees and customers to identify areas for improvement and refine your strategy accordingly.

By completing this activity, you'll be well on your way to developing a unified marketing strategy that drives success for both the franchisor and franchisees.

Looking Ahead

With a unified marketing strategy in place, you're ready to start implementing campaigns across different platforms. In the next chapters, we'll dive into the specifics of creating and managing Google Ads, optimising your Google Business Profile, and leveraging Facebook and Instagram Ads to reach your target audience. Each platform offers unique opportunities, and when used together as part of a cohesive strategy, they can help you achieve your marketing goals and grow your franchise.

Remember, a successful marketing strategy is not static—it evolves over time based on feedback, data, and changing market conditions. By staying agile and continuously refining your approach, you can ensure that your marketing efforts remain effective and aligned with your brand's objectives.

Chapter 4: Mastering Google Ads for Maximum ROI

Introduction

Google Ads is one of the most powerful tools in your digital marketing arsenal. It offers a unique opportunity to reach potential customers at the exact moment they are searching for products or services like yours. Whether you're a franchisee looking to drive local traffic to your business or a franchisor aiming to increase brand visibility across multiple locations, mastering Google Ads is crucial for achieving your marketing goals.

This chapter will guide you through the intricacies of Google Ads, from understanding the different types of campaigns to targeting the right audience and optimising your ads for maximum return on investment (ROI). We'll also explore advanced strategies for managing your ad spend and tracking the success of your campaigns. By the end of this chapter, you'll have the knowledge and tools you need to create effective Google Ads campaigns that deliver real results.

Understanding Google Ads Campaign Types

Google Ads offers several types of campaigns, each designed to achieve different objectives. Understanding these campaign types and when to use them is the first step in creating a successful Google Ads strategy.

1. Search Campaigns

Search campaigns are the most common type of Google Ads campaign. These ads appear in Google's search results when users search for keywords related to your business. For franchisees, search campaigns can be particularly effective for driving local traffic to your business by targeting users who are searching for products or services in your area.

- **Example:** A franchisee of a cleaning service might create a search campaign targeting keywords like "cleaning services near me" or "home cleaning in [city name]." When someone searches for these terms, the franchisee's ad will appear at the top of the search results, increasing the likelihood that the user will click on the ad and visit their website or call for more information.

2. Display Campaigns

Display campaigns allow you to place ads across Google's vast network of partner websites, known as the Google Display Network (GDN). These ads can appear as banners, images, or videos on websites that your target audience is likely to visit. Display campaigns are particularly useful for building brand awareness and reaching a broader audience.

- **Example:** A franchisor of a fitness brand might use display campaigns to run banner ads on health and wellness websites. These ads could feature images of the gym's facilities or promotional offers, encouraging users to learn more about the brand and visit their nearest location.

3. Shopping Campaigns

Shopping campaigns are ideal for businesses that sell products online. These ads appear in Google's search results with images, prices, and descriptions of your products. Shopping campaigns can drive online sales by making it easy for users to compare products and prices directly from the search results page.

- **Example:** A franchisee of a retail chain might use shopping campaigns to promote their online store. When someone searches for a specific product, such as "running shoes," the franchisee's ad will appear with an image of the shoes, the price, and a link to purchase them directly from the website.

4. Video Campaigns

Video campaigns allow you to advertise on YouTube and across Google's video partner sites. Video ads can be highly engaging and are an excellent way to showcase your brand's story, demonstrate your products, or share customer testimonials.

- **Example:** A franchisor of a quick-service restaurant chain might create a video campaign to promote a new menu item. The video ad could feature footage of the food being prepared and enjoyed, along with a call-to-action to visit the nearest location. These ads can be targeted to users who are watching food-related content on YouTube, ensuring that they reach an audience that is likely to be interested.

5. App Campaigns

If your business has a mobile app, app campaigns can help you drive downloads and engagement. These ads can appear across Google's platforms, including Search, Play, YouTube, and the Google Display Network.

- **Example:** A franchise with a loyalty app might use app campaigns to encourage customers to download the app and start earning rewards. The ad could highlight the benefits of the app, such as exclusive discounts or the ability to place orders ahead of time.

6. Local Campaigns

Local campaigns are designed to drive traffic to your physical locations. These ads can appear across Google's platforms, including Search, Maps, YouTube, and the Google Display Network. Local campaigns are particularly useful for franchisees who want to increase foot traffic and in-store sales.

- **Example:** A franchisee of a coffee shop might create a local campaign to promote a special offer, such as a free coffee with the purchase of a pastry. The ad would appear when users are searching for coffee shops in the area or when they are using Google Maps to find a nearby location.

Targeting the Right Audience

One of the biggest advantages of Google Ads is the ability to target your ads to specific audiences. By reaching the right people with the right message at the right time, you can maximise the effectiveness of your campaigns and increase your ROI.

1. Keyword Targeting

Keyword targeting is the foundation of search campaigns. It involves selecting the keywords that you want your ads to appear for when users search for them on Google. The key to successful keyword targeting is to choose keywords that are relevant to your business and that have the right balance of search volume and competition.

- **Broad Match:** This is the default keyword match type, where your ad can appear for searches that include any word in your keyword phrase, in any order. For example, if your keyword is "gym membership," your ad could appear for searches like "best gym membership deals" or "cheap memberships at local gyms."

- **Phrase Match:** Your ad will appear for searches that include your keyword phrase in the exact order you specify but may include additional words before or after. For example, "gym membership" could trigger ads for "affordable gym membership plans" but not "membership for gym classes."
- **Exact Match:** Your ad will only appear for searches that exactly match your keyword phrase, or close variations of it. This offers the most precise targeting. For example, "gym membership" would only trigger ads for searches like "gym membership" or "gym memberships" but not "membership at a gym."
- **Negative Keywords:** These are keywords for which you do not want your ads to appear. For instance, if you're a high-end fitness club, you might add "cheap" as a negative keyword to avoid showing your ads to users searching for low-cost options.

2. Geographic Targeting

Geographic targeting allows you to show your ads to users in specific locations. This is especially important for franchisees, who need to target customers within a certain radius of their physical location.

- **Radius Targeting:** You can set a radius around your business location, ensuring that your ads are only shown to users within that area. For example, a restaurant franchisee might target users within a 10-mile radius to attract local diners.
- **Location Groups:** You can target specific types of locations, such as universities, airports, or

shopping centres. For example, a retail franchise might target shoppers near a major mall to drive in-store traffic.

- **Local Extensions:** Adding local extensions to your ads can display your business address, phone number, and a map marker, making it easier for users to find and contact you. This is particularly effective for search and local campaigns.

3. Demographic Targeting

Demographic targeting allows you to target users based on factors such as age, gender, household income, and parental status. This can help you reach the audience that is most likely to be interested in your products or services.

- **Age and Gender:** If your products or services are more appealing to a specific age group or gender, you can adjust your bids to target these demographics more aggressively.
- **Household Income:** For businesses that offer premium products or services, targeting users with higher household incomes can be an effective strategy. Conversely, businesses that offer budget-friendly options might target lower-income households.
- **Parental Status:** If your business caters to families or parents, such as a children's clothing store or a family-friendly restaurant, targeting parents can help you reach a more relevant audience.

4. Interest and Behavioural Targeting

Google Ads allows you to target users based on their interests and online behaviours. This can help you reach an audience that is more likely to engage with your ads and convert.

- **Affinity Audiences:** These are users who have demonstrated a strong interest in a particular topic. For example, if you're a fitness franchise, you might target affinity audiences interested in "health and fitness" or "healthy eating."
- **In-Market Audiences:** These are users who are actively researching or planning to purchase a specific product or service. For example, if you're a home improvement franchise, you might target in-market audiences looking for "home renovation services" or "kitchen remodelling."
- **Custom Intent Audiences:** You can create custom audiences based on specific keywords and URLs that are relevant to your business. This allows you to target users who have shown intent to purchase products or services similar to yours.

5. Remarketing

Remarketing allows you to target users who have previously interacted with your website or ads. This is a powerful way to re-engage potential customers who didn't convert on their first visit.

- **Standard Remarketing:** Show ads to users who have visited your website but didn't take a desired action, such as making a purchase or filling out a contact form.
- **Dynamic Remarketing:** Show personalised ads to users based on the specific products or services they viewed on your website. For example, if a user browsed your online store for running shoes but didn't make a purchase, you can show them ads featuring the exact shoes they looked at.
- **Video Remarketing:** Target users who have interacted with your YouTube videos or channel, encouraging them to return to your site or watch more of your content.

Case Study: Effective Audience Targeting

Consider a case study of a franchisee who operates a local car wash. By using a combination of geographic, demographic, and interest-based targeting, the franchisee was able to create highly effective Google Ads campaigns that significantly increased business.

- **Geographic Targeting:** The franchisee set a 15-mile radius around the car wash location, ensuring that ads were only shown to users within driving distance.
- **Demographic Targeting:** The franchisee targeted users aged 25-45, based on data that showed this age group was most likely to use car wash services. They also targeted users with higher household incomes, as these customers were more likely to purchase premium services.
- **Interest Targeting:** The franchisee targeted users with an affinity for "automotive" and "car maintenance," ensuring that ads were shown to users who were already interested in taking care of their vehicles.

The result was a 35% increase in website visits and a 20% increase in on-site conversions, demonstrating the power of targeted Google Ads campaigns.

Optimising Your Google Ads Campaigns

Creating a Google Ads campaign is just the beginning. To maximise your ROI, you need to continuously optimise your campaigns based on performance data. This section will cover key optimisation strategies that can help you get the most out of your Google Ads investment.

1. Improving Ad Quality

Google uses a metric called Quality Score to determine the relevance and quality of your ads. A higher Quality Score can lead to better ad positions and lower costs per click (CPC). Here's how you can improve your Quality Score:

- **Ad Relevance:** Ensure that your ads are highly relevant to the keywords you're targeting. This includes writing ad copy that closely matches the user's search query.
- **Landing Page Experience:** The landing page that users are directed to after clicking your ad should be highly relevant to the ad itself. Ensure that the landing page loads quickly, is mobile-friendly, and provides the information or product the user is looking for.
- **Click-Through Rate (CTR):** A higher CTR indicates that your ads are relevant and compelling to users. Improve your CTR by testing different ad copy, using strong calls-to-action, and ensuring that your ads are visually appealing.

2. Managing Your Budget and Bids

Effective budget and bid management are crucial for maximising your ROI. Here are some strategies to consider:

- **Budget Allocation:** Allocate your budget based on the performance of different campaigns and ad groups. If a particular campaign is delivering a high ROI, consider increasing its budget to capitalise on its success.
- **Automated Bidding:** Google Ads offers several automated bidding strategies that can help you optimise your bids for specific goals, such as maximising conversions or targeting a specific cost per acquisition (CPA). Automated bidding

can save time and ensure that your bids are always optimised based on real-time data.
- **Bid Adjustments:** Use bid adjustments to increase or decrease your bids based on factors such as location, time of day, and device type. For example, if your data shows that users are more likely to convert during weekday mornings, you might increase your bids during those hours to capture more traffic.

3. A/B Testing

A/B testing, also known as split testing, involves comparing two versions of an ad or landing page to see which performs better. This is a powerful way to optimise your campaigns and improve your ROI.

- **Ad Copy:** Test different versions of your ad copy to see which one generates the highest CTR. For example, you might test two different headlines or calls-to-action to see which resonates more with your audience.
- **Landing Pages:** Test different landing page designs, headlines, and content to see which version results in the highest conversion rate. Even small changes, such as the colour of a button or the placement of a form, can have a significant impact on performance.
- **Audience Segments:** Test different audience segments to see which groups respond best to your ads. For example, you might test targeting users based on different interests or behaviours to see which segment delivers the highest ROI.

4. Monitoring and Reporting

Regularly monitoring and reporting on the performance of your Google Ads campaigns is essential for ongoing optimisation. Use the following metrics to track your progress and make data-driven decisions:

- **Impressions:** The number of times your ad was shown. This metric helps you understand the reach of your campaign.
- **Clicks:** The number of times users clicked on your ad. A higher number of clicks indicates that your ad is compelling and relevant to your audience.
- **Click-Through Rate (CTR):** The percentage of impressions that resulted in clicks. A higher CTR suggests that your ad is resonating with users.
- **Conversion Rate:** The percentage of clicks that resulted in a desired action, such as making a purchase or filling out a form. A higher conversion rate indicates that your landing page and offer are effective.
- **Cost Per Click (CPC):** The average amount you pay for each click. Monitoring your CPC helps you manage your budget and ensure that you're not overpaying for clicks.
- **Return on Ad Spend (ROAS):** The revenue generated from your ad campaign divided by the cost of the campaign. A higher ROAS indicates that your campaign is delivering a strong return on investment.

Case Study: Continuous Optimisation

Consider the case of a franchisee who operates a chain of hair salons. By continuously optimising their Google Ads campaigns, the franchisee was able to significantly improve their ROI over time.

- **Improving Ad Quality:** The franchisee focused on improving their ad relevance and landing page experience, resulting in a higher Quality Score and lower CPC. They also tested different ad copy and calls-to-action, which led to a 25% increase in CTR.

- **A/B Testing:** The franchisee conducted A/B tests on their landing pages, testing different headlines, images, and form placements. The winning version resulted in a 30% increase in conversion rate.
- **Monitoring and Reporting:** The franchisee regularly monitored key metrics, such as CTR, conversion rate, and ROAS. By making data-driven adjustments to their bids and budget allocation, they were able to increase their ROAS by 40% over six months.

This case study highlights the importance of continuous optimisation in achieving long-term success with Google Ads.

Advanced Google Ads Strategies

Once you have a solid foundation in Google Ads, you can start exploring more advanced strategies to take your campaigns to the next level. These strategies include:

1. Remarketing Lists for Search Ads (RLSA)

RLSA allows you to customise your search ads for users who have previously visited your website. This is a powerful way to re-engage potential customers who are already familiar with your brand.

- **Example:** A franchisee of a spa might use RLSA to target users who previously visited the website's booking page but didn't complete a booking. The ad could offer a special discount to incentivise them to return and complete the booking.

2. Customer Match

Customer Match allows you to target ads to your existing customers using data you've collected, such as email addresses or phone numbers. This is a great way to upsell or cross-sell to your customer base.

- **Example:** A franchisor of a home improvement brand might use Customer Match to target existing customers with ads for complementary products or services. For instance, if a customer previously purchased flooring, the ad could promote discounts on installation services.

3. Smart Campaigns

Smart campaigns are designed for small businesses and franchisees who want to automate their Google Ads management. These campaigns use machine learning to optimise your ads and targeting automatically.

- **Example:** A franchisee who operates a local pet grooming service might use a Smart campaign to automate their Google Ads, allowing them to focus on running their business while Google optimises the campaign for the best results.

4. Google Ads Scripts

Google Ads Scripts are a powerful tool for automating and managing your campaigns. They allow you to automate tasks such as bid adjustments, budget management, and reporting.

- **Example:** A franchisor might use Google Ads Scripts to automatically pause underperforming ads and allocate more budget to high-performing campaigns. This ensures that the campaign is always optimised for maximum ROI.

Activity: Launching and Optimising Your Google Ads Campaigns

Now that you've learned about the different types of Google Ads campaigns and strategies for optimising them, it's time to put that knowledge into action. This activity will guide you through the process of launching and optimising your Google Ads campaigns.

1. **Choose Your Campaign Type:**
   o Based on your business goals, choose the most appropriate Google Ads campaign type. If you're looking to drive local traffic, consider a search or local campaign. If you're focused on brand awareness, a display or video campaign might be more effective.
2. **Define Your Target Audience:**
   o Use the targeting options available in Google Ads to define your audience. Consider factors such as keywords, geographic location, demographics, and interests. Be sure to include negative keywords to avoid wasting ad spend on irrelevant searches.
3. **Create Compelling Ads:**
   o Write ad copy that is clear, concise, and compelling. Highlight your unique selling proposition and include a strong call-to-action. Be sure to use high-quality images or videos if you're running a display or video campaign.
4. **Set Your Budget and Bids:**
   o Determine your daily budget and bid strategy. Consider using automated bidding to optimise your bids based on real-time data. Monitor your budget

regularly to ensure that you're not overspending.

5. **Launch Your Campaign:**
   - Once your campaign is set up, launch it and start monitoring its performance. Use Google Ads' reporting tools to track key metrics such as CTR, conversion rate, and ROAS.

6. **Optimise for Performance:**
   - Continuously optimise your campaign based on performance data. Conduct A/B tests, adjust your bids and budget, and refine your targeting to improve your results. Regularly monitor your Quality Score and make improvements to your ad relevance and landing page experience.

7. **Advanced Techniques:**
   - Once you're comfortable with the basics, start exploring advanced techniques such as RLSA, Customer Match, and Google Ads Scripts. These tools can help you take your campaigns to the next level and maximise your ROI.

By completing this activity, you'll be well on your way to mastering Google Ads and creating campaigns that deliver real results for your business.

Looking Ahead

Now that you've learned how to create and optimise Google Ads campaigns, you're ready to explore other digital marketing platforms that can complement your efforts. In the next chapters, we'll dive into the specifics of optimising your Google Business Profile and leveraging Facebook and Instagram Ads to reach your target audience. By integrating these platforms into a cohesive marketing strategy, you can maximise your reach and achieve your business goals.

Remember, success with Google Ads is not a one-time effort—it requires continuous learning, experimentation, and optimisation. By staying informed about the latest trends and best practices, you can ensure that your Google Ads campaigns remain effective and aligned with your overall marketing strategy.

Chapter 5: Harnessing the Power of Google Business Profiles

Introduction

In the digital age, your Google Business Profile (GBP) often serves as the first point of contact between your business and potential customers. A well-optimised GBP can be a powerful tool for driving local traffic, improving your visibility in search results, and enhancing your brand's credibility. For franchisees and franchisors alike, mastering the nuances of Google Business Profiles is essential for local SEO success and maintaining a strong, consistent online presence.

This chapter will guide you through the process of setting up, optimising, and managing your Google Business Profile. We'll explore advanced features such as posts, reviews, and insights, and we'll provide strategies for managing multiple locations within a franchise. By the end of this chapter, you'll have the knowledge and tools you need to make the most of your Google Business Profile and drive real business results.

The Importance of Google Business Profiles in Local SEO

Google Business Profiles play a crucial role in local search engine optimisation (SEO). When potential customers search for businesses like yours on Google, your GBP helps determine whether your business appears in local search results, including the highly coveted "Local Pack" and Google Maps.

1. What is Local SEO?

Local SEO is the process of optimising your online presence to attract more business from relevant local searches. These searches typically include location-specific keywords, such as "coffee shop near me" or "best pizza in [city name]." For franchisees, local SEO is vital because it helps you reach customers in your immediate vicinity who are actively looking for your products or services.

Google Business Profiles are central to local SEO because they provide Google with critical information about your business, such as your address, phone number, hours of operation, and customer reviews. When properly optimised, your GBP can help you rank higher in local search results, making it easier for customers to find and choose your business.

2. The Local Pack and Google Maps

One of the most prominent features of local search results is the "Local Pack," a section that highlights the top three local businesses related to a user's search query. The Local Pack appears at the top of the search results page, above organic listings, making it a prime spot for attracting clicks and driving traffic.

Your Google Business Profile is a key factor in determining whether your business appears in the Local Pack. Factors such as relevance, distance, and prominence influence your placement in the Local Pack, and optimising your GBP can improve your chances of securing one of these coveted spots.

Google Maps is another important component of local SEO. When users search for a business or service on Google Maps, the results are largely based on the information provided in Google Business Profiles. Ensuring that your profile is complete, accurate, and optimised can help you rank higher in Google Maps searches and attract more customers to your physical location.

Case Study: The Impact of Local SEO

Consider a franchisee who operates a local bakery in a competitive market. By focusing on optimising their Google Business Profile, the franchisee was able to significantly improve their visibility in local search results.

- **Complete Profile:** The franchisee ensured that their GBP was fully completed with accurate information, high-quality photos, and a detailed description of the bakery's offerings.
- **Consistent Updates:** They regularly updated their profile with new photos, posts about seasonal products, and changes to their hours of operation.
- **Encouraging Reviews:** The franchisee encouraged satisfied customers to leave positive reviews, which helped build credibility and improve their profile's prominence in search results.

As a result of these efforts, the bakery's GBP consistently appeared in the Local Pack for relevant search queries, such as "best bakery near me" and "fresh bread in [city name]." This increased visibility led to a 40% increase in foot traffic and a 25% boost in sales over six months.

Setting Up Your Google Business Profile

Setting up your Google Business Profile is the first step in optimising your local SEO. Whether you're creating a new profile or claiming an existing one, it's important to provide accurate and comprehensive information.

1. Creating or Claiming Your Profile

If you haven't already claimed your Google Business Profile, you'll need to do so before you can manage and optimise it.

- **Step 1:** Visit Google Business Profile and sign in with your Google account. If you don't already have an account, you'll need to create one.
- **Step 2:** Enter your business name. If your business is already listed on Google, you'll see it in the search results. Select your business and click "Claim this business." If your business isn't listed, you can create a new profile by entering your business details.
- **Step 3:** Choose the appropriate business category. It's important to select the category that best describes your business, as this will help Google match your profile with relevant search queries.
- **Step 4:** Verify your business. Google will send you a verification code by mail, phone, or email. This step is crucial, as it confirms that you are the rightful owner of the business and gives you control over the profile.

2. Completing Your Profile Information

Once you've claimed your profile, the next step is to ensure that all your business information is complete and accurate.

- **Business Name:** Ensure that your business name is entered exactly as it appears in the real world. Avoid adding extra keywords or location details to your business name, as this can violate Google's guidelines and result in penalties.
- **Address:** Enter your full business address, including street name, city, and postcode. If your business has multiple locations, each location

should have its own profile with a unique address.

- **Phone Number:** Provide a phone number that customers can use to contact your business. If possible, use a local phone number rather than a toll-free number, as this can improve your local SEO.
- **Website:** Include a link to your business's website. If your business has multiple locations, consider linking to a location-specific landing page rather than the homepage.
- **Business Hours:** Enter your regular business hours, as well as any special hours for holidays or events. Keeping your hours up to date is important for ensuring that customers know when your business is open.
- **Category:** Ensure that your business category accurately reflects what your business offers. You can also add secondary categories if your business falls into multiple categories.
- **Attributes:** Attributes allow you to provide additional information about your business, such as whether you offer free Wi-Fi, wheelchair accessibility, or outdoor seating. Adding relevant attributes can help your profile stand out to customers.

3. Adding Photos and Videos

Visual content is a powerful way to enhance your Google Business Profile and attract more customers. Profiles with high-quality photos and videos receive more views and engagement than those without.

- **Exterior Photos:** Upload photos of the exterior of your business, including your signage and entrance. This helps customers recognise your location when they visit.

- **Interior Photos:** Show off the interior of your business, including the décor, seating areas, and any unique features. This gives customers a sense of what to expect when they visit.
- **Product Photos:** If you sell products, upload photos of your best-selling items or new arrivals. Make sure the photos are well-lit and showcase the products in an appealing way.
- **Team Photos:** Introduce your team by uploading photos of your staff. This can help personalise your business and make customers feel more connected to your brand.
- **Videos:** Consider adding short videos that highlight your business, such as a virtual tour, customer testimonials, or a behind-the-scenes look at how your products are made. Videos can be more engaging than photos and provide a dynamic way to showcase your business.

4. Crafting a Compelling Business Description

Your business description is an opportunity to tell potential customers what makes your business unique and why they should choose you over the competition.

- **Keep it Concise:** Google allows up to 750 characters for your business description, but it's important to be concise and to the point. Focus on the most important aspects of your business and what sets you apart.
- **Highlight Your USP:** Your Unique Selling Proposition (USP) should be front and centre in your description. Whether it's your exceptional customer service, innovative products, or convenient location, make sure customers know what makes your business special.
- **Include Keywords:** While your business description shouldn't be overly keyword-stuffed, it's a good idea to include a few relevant

keywords that describe your business. This can help improve your profile's visibility in search results.

Leveraging Google Business Profile Features

Google Business Profiles offer a range of features that can enhance your profile and help you engage with customers. By taking full advantage of these features, you can improve your local SEO and provide a better experience for potential customers.

1. Posts

Google Business Profile posts allow you to share updates, promotions, events, and more directly on your profile. Posts appear in your profile on both Google Search and Google Maps, making them a valuable tool for keeping customers informed and engaged.

- **Types of Posts:**
  - **What's New:** Share general updates about your business, such as new products, services, or changes to your operations.
  - **Events:** Promote upcoming events, such as sales, workshops, or special promotions. Be sure to include the date, time, and location of the event.
  - **Offers:** Highlight special offers or discounts. Include details about the offer, such as the discount amount, terms and conditions, and expiration date.
  - **COVID-19 Updates:** If your business is affected by the COVID-19 pandemic, you can use this post type to share updates on changes to your operations, safety measures, or new services such as curb side pickup.

- **Best Practices for Posts:**
  - **Be Timely:** Posts are most effective when they're relevant and timely. Use posts to promote current events, seasonal offers, or important updates.
  - **Include a Call-to-Action:** Encourage customers to take action by including a call-to-action (CTA) in your post. This could be something like "Learn More," "Call Now," or "Visit Us Today."
  - **Use High-Quality Images:** Posts with images are more likely to catch the attention of users. Use high-quality, relevant images that support the content of your post.

2. Reviews and Reputation Management

Customer reviews are a critical component of your Google Business Profile. Not only do reviews influence potential customers' decisions, but they also impact your profile's prominence in search results.

- **Encouraging Positive Reviews:**
  - **Ask for Reviews:** Encourage satisfied customers to leave positive reviews by asking them directly. You can do this in person, through email, or by including a review request in your follow-up communications.
  - **Make it Easy:** Provide customers with a direct link to your Google Business Profile where they can leave a review. The easier you make it for customers to leave a review, the more likely they are to do so.
  - **Incentivise Reviews:** Consider offering a small incentive, such as a discount or freebie, to customers who leave a review. Just be sure to follow Google's guidelines

and avoid incentivising positive reviews only.

- **Responding to Reviews:**
  - ○ **Positive Reviews:** Always thank customers for leaving positive reviews. A simple "Thank you for your feedback!" can go a long way in showing your appreciation.
  - ○ **Negative Reviews:** Responding to negative reviews is just as important, if not more so. Address the customer's concerns, apologise if necessary, and offer to resolve the issue. Your response should be professional and courteous, even if the review is unfair.
- **Monitoring Your Reviews:**
  - ○ **Review Alerts:** Set up alerts to notify you whenever a new review is posted. This ensures that you can respond promptly to both positive and negative feedback.
  - ○ **Analyse Review Trends:** Regularly analyse your reviews to identify trends or recurring issues. For example, if multiple customers mention slow service, it may be an area where you need to improve.

3. Insights and Analytics

Google Business Profile provides valuable insights into how customers are interacting with your profile. These insights can help you understand what's working and where there's room for improvement.

- **Key Metrics:**
  - ○ **Search Queries:** See the search terms customers used to find your profile. This can help you understand what keywords are driving traffic to your profile and

whether there are additional keywords you should target.

- o **Views:** Track the number of times your profile was viewed in Google Search and Maps. A higher number of views indicates greater visibility.
- o **Actions:** Monitor the actions customers take on your profile, such as visiting your website, calling your business, or requesting directions. These metrics can help you gauge how effectively your profile is driving engagement.

- **Using Insights to Improve Your Profile:**
  - o **Refine Your Keywords:** If certain search queries are driving a lot of traffic to your profile, consider incorporating those keywords into your business description, posts, or website content.
  - o **Optimise Your Photos:** If photos are receiving a lot of views, make sure they're showcasing your business in the best light. If certain types of photos are more popular, consider adding more of those.
  - o **Enhance Your Posts:** If certain types of posts are driving more engagement, consider creating similar content in the future. Experiment with different post types, images, and CTAs to see what resonates most with your audience.

Case Study: Maximising the Use of Google Business Profile Features

Consider a franchisee who operates a local pet grooming service. By leveraging the full range of features offered by Google Business Profile, the franchisee was able to significantly increase visibility and customer engagement.

- **Regular Posts:** The franchisee used the "What's New" post type to share updates on new grooming packages and seasonal promotions. They also used the "Events" post type to promote special grooming events, such as "Puppy Spa Day."
- **Encouraging Reviews:** After each grooming appointment, the franchisee asked customers to leave a review on their Google Business Profile. They also included a link to the review page in their follow-up emails.
- **Responding to Reviews:** The franchisee responded promptly to all reviews, thanking customers for positive feedback and addressing any concerns raised in negative reviews. This helped build a positive reputation and encouraged more customers to leave reviews.
- **Monitoring Insights:** The franchisee regularly monitored their profile's insights to track the effectiveness of their posts and the search queries that were driving the most traffic. They used this data to refine their keyword strategy and create more targeted posts.

As a result of these efforts, the pet grooming service saw a 50% increase in profile views and a 30% increase in customer calls within three months. The franchisee also noticed a significant improvement in their profile's ranking in local search results, helping them attract more customers.

Managing Multiple Locations

For franchisors and franchisees managing multiple locations, maintaining consistent and optimised Google Business Profiles across all locations is crucial. Here's how to effectively manage multiple locations within a franchise:

1. Bulk Location Management

Google offers tools for managing multiple locations simultaneously, which is particularly useful for franchisors with a large number of locations.

- **Bulk Verification:** If you have 10 or more locations, you can apply for bulk verification, which allows you to verify all your locations at once rather than individually.
- **Bulk Upload:** You can upload and manage multiple locations using a spreadsheet. This allows you to update information for all your locations in one go, ensuring consistency across the board.
- **Location Groups:** Organise your locations into groups based on region, type, or other criteria. This makes it easier to manage specific sets of locations and apply changes uniformly.

2. Ensuring Consistency

Consistency is key when managing multiple locations. Here are some tips to ensure that all your locations are represented consistently on Google:

- **Standardise Information:** Use the same format for business names, addresses, phone numbers, and other details across all locations. This helps avoid confusion and ensures that customers receive accurate information.
- **Use the Same Branding:** Ensure that all locations use the same logos, colours, and branding elements in their profiles. This helps maintain a cohesive brand image across all locations.
- **Train Local Managers:** Provide training to local managers on how to manage their location's Google Business Profile. Ensure that they

understand the importance of keeping information up to date and responding to customer reviews.

3. Localising Content

While consistency is important, it's also essential to tailor content to each location. Here's how to localise your Google Business Profiles:

- **Localised Descriptions:** Consider adding location-specific details to each profile's business description. For example, you might mention landmarks near the location or highlight services that are particularly popular in that area.
- **Local Photos:** Use photos that showcase the unique features of each location. For example, a restaurant franchise might upload photos of each location's interior décor and popular dishes.
- **Local Posts:** Create posts that are relevant to each location's audience. For example, you might promote a local event or offer a discount to customers who visit during a community festival.

Case Study: Managing Multiple Locations

A franchisor of a national fitness chain successfully managed the Google Business Profiles for over 100 locations by implementing a consistent yet localised approach.

- **Bulk Upload:** The franchisor used Google's bulk upload tool to create and manage profiles for all locations, ensuring that each profile had consistent information and branding.
- **Localised Content:** Each location's profile included a localised business description and photos that highlighted the unique features of the

gym, such as specialised equipment or local events.

- **Centralised Management:** While local managers were responsible for day-to-day updates and responding to reviews, the franchisor provided regular training and support to ensure consistency across all profiles.

As a result of these efforts, the fitness chain saw improved visibility in local search results across multiple markets. The consistent yet localised approach also helped build a strong, cohesive brand image that resonated with customers nationwide.

Activity: Optimising Your Google Business Profile

Now that you understand the importance of Google Business Profiles and how to leverage their features, it's time to optimise your own profile. This activity will guide you through the process of setting up, enhancing, and managing your GBP.

1. **Claim or Create Your Profile:**
   - If you haven't already done so, claim or create your Google Business Profile. Follow the steps outlined in this chapter to verify your business and ensure that all information is accurate.
2. **Complete Your Profile Information:**
   - Ensure that your business name, address, phone number, website, and business hours are all correctly entered. Double-check for consistency with other online listings.
3. **Add High-Quality Photos:**
   - Upload a variety of high-quality photos, including exterior and interior shots, product photos, and team photos.

Consider adding a short video to
showcase your business.
4. **Craft a Compelling Description:**
    o Write a concise and compelling business
    description that highlights your USP and
    includes relevant keywords. Make sure it
    accurately reflects what your business
    offers.
5. **Leverage GBP Features:**
    o Start using Google Business Profile
    features such as posts and reviews.
    Create a post to promote a current offer
    or event and respond to any recent
    reviews.
6. **Monitor Insights:**
    o Use the insights provided by Google to
    track the performance of your profile. Pay
    attention to metrics such as search
    queries, views, and customer actions. Use
    this data to refine your profile and make
    informed decisions.
7. **Manage Multiple Locations:**
    o If you're managing multiple locations,
    ensure that all profiles are consistent and
    localised where appropriate. Use
    Google's bulk management tools to
    streamline the process.

By completing this activity, you'll be well on your way to
optimising your Google Business Profile and improving
your local SEO. An optimised GBP can help you attract
more customers, increase foot traffic, and enhance your
overall online presence.

Looking Ahead

With your Google Business Profile optimised and fully
functional, you're now ready to explore other powerful
digital marketing tools. In the next chapters, we'll dive
into the world of Facebook and Instagram Ads, where

you'll learn how to create and manage campaigns that drive engagement, build brand awareness, and generate leads.

Remember, your Google Business Profile is a dynamic tool that requires regular updates and maintenance. By staying proactive and continually optimising your profile, you can ensure that your business remains visible and attractive to potential customers in your local area.

Chapter 6: Leveraging Facebook Ads for Business Growth

Introduction

Facebook Ads offers one of the most robust and versatile platforms for reaching your target audience and driving business growth. With over 2.8 billion monthly active users, Facebook provides a vast audience that businesses can tap into with highly targeted advertising. Whether you're a franchisee aiming to increase foot traffic at your local store or a franchisor looking to build brand awareness across multiple locations, Facebook Ads can be a powerful tool in your digital marketing arsenal.

This chapter will explore the ins and outs of Facebook Ads, from setting up your first campaign to advanced targeting strategies and ad formats. We'll also delve into how to measure the success of your campaigns and continuously optimise them for better results. By the end of this chapter, you'll have the knowledge and confidence to create effective Facebook Ads that drive real business outcomes.

Understanding the Facebook Ads Platform

Before diving into campaign creation, it's essential to understand the Facebook Ads platform and its unique features. Facebook Ads operates through the Facebook Ads Manager, a comprehensive tool that allows you to create, manage, and optimise your ads. Understanding how the platform works will enable you to make the most of its capabilities.

1. The Facebook Ads Manager

Facebook Ads Manager is the hub where all your Facebook advertising activities are managed. It provides a range of tools for creating ads, setting budgets, targeting audiences, and tracking performance.

- **Campaign Structure:** Facebook Ads Manager organises your advertising efforts into three levels: Campaigns, Ad Sets, and Ads.
  - **Campaign:** The campaign level is where you define your objective, such as brand awareness, traffic, or conversions. Each campaign can have multiple ad sets and ads under it.
  - **Ad Set:** At the ad set level, you determine your targeting options, budget, schedule, and placements. Ad sets allow you to segment your audience and test different targeting strategies.
  - **Ad:** The ad level is where you create the actual ad content, including the ad copy, images, videos, and call-to-action. You can have multiple ads within each ad set.
- **Key Features of Ads Manager:**
  - **Audience Insights:** This tool helps you understand your target audience's demographics, interests, and behaviours, allowing you to refine your targeting.
  - **Creative Hub:** A tool for designing and previewing ads across different placements and formats.
  - **Ad Reporting:** Provides detailed analytics on your ad performance, including metrics like reach, engagement, conversions, and return on ad spend (ROAS).

2. Facebook Pixel

The Facebook Pixel is a piece of code that you place on your website to track user interactions and measure the effectiveness of your ads. By setting up the Facebook

Pixel, you can track actions such as page views, purchases, and form submissions, allowing you to optimise your ads for better results.

- **Benefits of Using Facebook Pixel:**
    - **Conversion Tracking:** See how users interact with your website after clicking on your Facebook ad.
    - **Retargeting:** Create custom audiences based on users who have visited your website but didn't convert, allowing you to re-engage them with targeted ads.
    - **Lookalike Audiences:** Use the data collected by the Pixel to create lookalike audiences, which are new audiences that share similar characteristics with your existing customers.

3. Ad Objectives

Facebook Ads offers a variety of campaign objectives, each designed to help you achieve specific business goals. Choosing the right objective is crucial for the success of your campaign.

- **Awareness Objectives:** Designed to generate interest in your business.
    - **Brand Awareness:** Increase awareness of your brand by reaching people who are more likely to be interested.
    - **Reach:** Show your ad to as many people as possible within your target audience.
- **Consideration Objectives:** Encourage people to learn more about your business.
    - **Traffic:** Drive users to your website, app, or Facebook page.
    - **Engagement:** Increase engagement with your content, such as likes, comments, and shares.

- o **App Installs:** Encourage users to download and install your app.
- o **Video Views:** Promote videos to raise awareness or educate your audience.
- o **Lead Generation:** Collect leads, such as email addresses, directly within Facebook.
- **Conversion Objectives:** Encourage people to take specific actions, such as making a purchase.
  - o **Conversions:** Drive valuable actions on your website, app, or Messenger.
  - o **Catalogue Sales:** Promote products from your catalogue to generate sales.
  - o **Store Traffic:** Drive visits to your physical locations.

Case Study: Selecting the Right Objective

A franchisee of a fast-casual dining chain wanted to increase lunchtime traffic at their location. After reviewing the available objectives, they chose the "Store Traffic" objective to drive local customers to their restaurant.

- **Campaign Setup:** The franchisee created a campaign using the Store Traffic objective, targeting users within a 5-mile radius of their location. They used a combination of interest-based and demographic targeting to reach potential customers who were likely to be interested in dining out during lunch hours.
- **Ad Creative:** The ad featured an enticing image of the restaurant's lunch specials, with a call-to-action to "Visit Us Today!" The ad also included the restaurant's address and a map showing the location.
- **Results:** The campaign resulted in a 20% increase in lunchtime traffic over the course of a month, demonstrating the effectiveness of choosing the right objective for the campaign's goals.

Setting Up Your First Facebook Ads Campaign

Now that you understand the basics of the Facebook Ads platform, it's time to set up your first campaign. This section will guide you through the process, from selecting your objective to creating compelling ad content.

1. Define Your Campaign Objective

The first step in creating a Facebook Ads campaign is to define your objective. Consider what you want to achieve with your campaign—whether it's driving traffic to your website, generating leads, or increasing brand awareness—and select the appropriate objective in Facebook Ads Manager.

- **Example:** A franchisee of a local fitness centre wants to attract new members to their gym. They choose the "Lead Generation" objective, as they want to collect contact information from potential customers who are interested in signing up for a free trial.

2. Set Up Your Ad Set

Once you've selected your objective, the next step is to set up your ad set. This involves defining your target audience, budget, schedule, and placements.

- **Audience Targeting:** Define your target audience based on demographics, interests, and behaviours. Consider factors such as age, gender, location, and interests that align with your ideal customer profile.
    - ○ **Example:** The fitness centre franchisee targets individuals aged 25-45 within a 10-

mile radius of the gym who are interested in fitness, health, and wellness.

- **Budget and Schedule:** Set your daily or lifetime budget and determine how long you want your ads to run. Facebook Ads Manager allows you to schedule your ads to run at specific times or continuously until your budget is exhausted.
    - o **Example:** The franchisee sets a daily budget of £50 and schedules the ads to run during the morning and evening hours, when people are most likely to be thinking about their fitness routines.
- **Placements:** Choose where you want your ads to appear, such as in the Facebook News Feed, Instagram Feed, Stories, or Audience Network. You can also use automatic placements, which allows Facebook to place your ads where they are most likely to perform well.
    - o **Example:** The franchisee selects automatic placements to allow Facebook to optimise the ad delivery across Facebook and Instagram.

3. Create Your Ad Content

With your ad set defined, it's time to create the ad content itself. This involves crafting compelling ad copy, choosing eye-catching images or videos, and including a strong call-to-action.

- **Ad Format:** Choose the format that best suits your campaign objectives, such as single image, video, carousel, or slideshow ads.
    - o **Example:** The fitness centre franchisee chooses a video ad format to showcase the gym's facilities and highlight the benefits of membership.
- **Ad Copy:** Write clear and concise ad copy that conveys your message and encourages users to

take action. Focus on the benefits of your offer and what sets your business apart.

- Example: The ad copy for the fitness centre reads: "Get fit and feel great with our 7-day free trial! Sign up now and experience our state-of-the-art facilities and expert trainers."

- **Call-to-Action (CTA):** Include a CTA that directs users to take the next step, such as "Sign Up," "Learn More," or "Shop Now."
  - **Example:** The fitness centre ad includes a CTA button that says, "Sign Up," directing users to a lead generation form where they can enter their contact information.

Case Study: Creating Compelling Ad Content

A franchisee of a children's educational franchise wanted to promote their upcoming summer camp program. They used a combination of video and carousel ads to showcase the camp's activities and encourage parents to sign up.

- **Ad Format:** The franchisee chose a carousel ad format, featuring multiple images of different camp activities, such as arts and crafts, science experiments, and outdoor games. Each image included a brief description of the activity.
- **Ad Copy:** The ad copy highlighted the benefits of the summer camp, such as hands-on learning, fun-filled days, and the opportunity for children to make new friends. The franchisee also included a limited-time discount for early sign-ups.
- **Call-to-Action:** The CTA button read "Register Now," directing parents to a landing page where they could learn more about the camp and complete the registration process.

The campaign was a success, resulting in a 30% increase in registrations compared to the previous year. The combination of engaging visuals, clear messaging, and a strong CTA helped drive conversions and achieve the campaign's goals.

Advanced Targeting Strategies

Once you're comfortable with the basics of Facebook Ads, you can start exploring more advanced targeting strategies to reach a highly relevant audience. These strategies include Custom Audiences, Lookalike Audiences, and detailed interest targeting.

1. Custom Audiences

Custom Audiences allow you to target ads to people who have already interacted with your business, whether through your website, app, or customer list. This is a powerful way to re-engage existing customers or users who are already familiar with your brand.

- **Website Custom Audiences:** Use the Facebook Pixel to create audiences based on users who have visited specific pages on your website or taken certain actions, such as adding a product to their cart but not completing the purchase.
  - **Example:** A franchisee of an online clothing store creates a Custom Audience of users who viewed a specific product page but didn't make a purchase. They then run a retargeting ad offering a discount on that product.
- **Customer List Custom Audiences:** Upload a list of your existing customers, such as email subscribers or past buyers, to create a Custom Audience. Facebook matches the data with user profiles, allowing you to target ads to these individuals.

- ○ **Example:** A franchisor of a national restaurant chain uploads a list of loyalty program members and targets them with ads promoting a new menu item.
- **Engagement Custom Audiences:** Create audiences based on users who have interacted with your content on Facebook or Instagram, such as watching a video, liking a post, or clicking on an ad.
  - ○ **Example:** A franchisee of a fitness brand creates a Custom Audience of users who watched at least 50% of a workout video on Instagram. They then target these users with an ad promoting a fitness class package.

2. Lookalike Audiences

Lookalike Audiences allow you to reach new people who are similar to your existing customers. By using data from your Custom Audiences, Facebook identifies users who share similar characteristics and behaviours, making them more likely to be interested in your business.

- **Creating Lookalike Audiences:** To create a Lookalike Audience, you'll first need a source audience, such as a Custom Audience or a list of your best customers. Facebook then finds users who closely match the characteristics of this source audience.
  - ○ **Example:** A franchisor of a home services company creates a Lookalike Audience based on their top 10% of customers who have booked services through their website. They use this Lookalike Audience to run a campaign promoting a seasonal service package.
- **Refining Lookalike Audiences:** You can refine your Lookalike Audience by adjusting the

percentage of similarity. A 1% Lookalike Audience will closely match your source audience, while a 5% Lookalike Audience will be broader but less precise.

- o **Example:** A franchisee of a luxury spa creates a 1% Lookalike Audience to target users who are highly similar to their existing high-value customers, focusing on promoting premium spa packages.

3. Detailed Interest Targeting

Detailed interest targeting allows you to target users based on their interests, activities, and behaviours. This can help you reach a highly specific audience that aligns with your business's products or services.

- **Interest Categories:** Facebook offers a wide range of interest categories, such as fitness, travel, fashion, technology, and more. You can select multiple interests to narrow down your audience.
  - o **Example:** A franchisee of a travel agency targets users interested in "adventure travel," "beach holidays," and "luxury resorts" to promote a range of vacation packages.
- **Behavioural Targeting:** In addition to interests, you can target users based on their online and offline behaviours, such as purchasing habits, device usage, and travel patterns.
  - o **Example:** A franchisor of an e-commerce brand targets users who have made online purchases in the past 30 days, promoting a flash sale event.

Case Study: Advanced Targeting for Better Results

A franchisee of a high-end jewellery store wanted to increase sales during the holiday season. They used a combination of Custom Audiences, Lookalike Audiences, and detailed interest targeting to reach a highly relevant audience.

- **Custom Audience:** The franchisee created a Custom Audience of users who had visited their website's product pages but hadn't completed a purchase. They retargeted these users with ads promoting holiday discounts on popular items.
- **Lookalike Audience:** They also created a 1% Lookalike Audience based on their top customers, targeting users who were likely to be interested in high-end jewellery.
- **Interest Targeting:** To further refine their audience, the franchisee targeted users interested in "luxury goods," "fashion," and "gifts for her."

The advanced targeting strategy resulted in a 35% increase in online sales and a 20% increase in in-store visits during the holiday season. The combination of retargeting, Lookalike Audiences, and interest targeting helped the franchisee reach a highly engaged audience and maximise their campaign's effectiveness.

Measuring Success and Optimising Campaigns

Creating and launching a Facebook Ads campaign is only the beginning. To ensure your campaigns are delivering the desired results, it's essential to monitor performance, measure success, and continuously optimise your ads.

1. Key Metrics to Track

Facebook Ads Manager provides a wealth of data on your campaign's performance. Here are some key metrics to track:

- **Reach:** The number of unique users who saw your ad. A higher reach indicates that your ad is being shown to a large audience.
- **Impressions:** The total number of times your ad was shown. Multiple impressions can occur when a user sees your ad more than once.
- **Click-Through Rate (CTR):** The percentage of users who clicked on your ad after seeing it. A higher CTR suggests that your ad is relevant and compelling to your audience.
- **Cost Per Click (CPC):** The average cost you pay for each click on your ad. Monitoring your CPC helps you manage your budget and ensure that you're not overpaying for clicks.
- **Conversions:** The number of desired actions taken by users, such as making a purchase, signing up for a newsletter, or downloading an app. Conversions are the ultimate measure of your campaign's success.
- **Return on Ad Spend (ROAS):** The revenue generated from your ad campaign divided by the cost of the campaign. A higher ROAS indicates that your campaign is delivering a strong return on investment.

2. A/B Testing and Experimentation

A/B testing, also known as split testing, is a powerful method for optimising your Facebook Ads campaigns. By testing different versions of your ads, you can determine which elements are most effective and make data-driven decisions to improve performance.

- **Ad Copy:** Test different headlines, body text, and calls-to-action to see which combination generates the highest CTR and conversions.
  - ○ **Example:** A franchisee of a local beauty salon tests two different headlines: "Pamper Yourself with Our Luxury Treatments" vs. "Get 20% Off Your First Visit." The A/B test reveals that the discount offer generates a higher CTR, leading the franchisee to use that headline in future ads.
- **Ad Creative:** Experiment with different images, videos, and ad formats to see which visuals resonate most with your audience.
  - ○ **Example:** A franchisor of a home improvement brand tests a single image ad against a video ad showcasing a kitchen remodel. The video ad outperforms the image ad, leading the franchisor to invest more in video content.
- **Audience Segments:** Test different audience segments, such as age groups, interests, or behaviours, to identify the most responsive demographic.
  - ○ **Example:** A franchisee of a family-friendly restaurant tests ads targeting parents with young children vs. ads targeting older adults. The test reveals that parents are more likely to engage with the ads, prompting the franchisee to focus on family-oriented messaging.

3. Budget and Bid Optimisation

Optimising your budget and bids is crucial for maximising the effectiveness of your Facebook Ads campaigns. Here are some strategies to consider:

- **Budget Allocation:** Allocate more budget to high-performing ad sets and reduce or pause low-performing ones. Use Facebook's reporting tools to identify which ad sets are delivering the best results.
  - **Example:** A franchisee of a pet grooming service notices that ads targeting pet owners with small dogs are performing better than those targeting large dog owners. They allocate more budget to the small dog audience to maximise conversions.
- **Bid Strategies:** Experiment with different bid strategies, such as lowest cost, cost cap, or bid cap, to find the one that delivers the best results for your campaign objectives.
  - **Example:** A franchisor of a national retail chain tests a cost cap strategy to control the maximum amount they're willing to pay for conversions. This strategy helps them stay within their budget while achieving a higher ROAS.
- **Ad Scheduling:** Use Facebook's ad scheduling feature to show your ads at times when your audience is most active and likely to convert. This can help reduce wasted spend and improve performance.
  - **Example:** A franchisee of a coffee shop schedules their ads to run in the early morning and late afternoon, when people are most likely to be thinking about coffee. This targeted scheduling results in a higher CTR and more in-store visits.

Case Study: Continuous Optimisation for Better Results

A franchisee of a home cleaning service wanted to improve the performance of their Facebook Ads campaign. By implementing A/B testing, budget optimisation, and ad scheduling, they were able to achieve significant improvements.

- **A/B Testing:** The franchisee tested different ad creatives, including a before-and-after image of a cleaned room vs. a video showcasing the cleaning process. The video ad generated a 25% higher CTR, so they shifted their focus to video content.
- **Budget Optimisation:** The franchisee reallocated their budget to focus on the best-performing ad sets, which targeted working professionals and parents with young children. This resulted in a 30% increase in conversions.
- **Ad Scheduling:** By scheduling ads to run during the evening hours, when their target audience was most likely to be at home and thinking about cleaning services, the franchisee achieved a 20% reduction in CPC and a higher conversion rate.

Through continuous optimisation, the franchisee was able to double their ROAS and significantly increase the effectiveness of their Facebook Ads campaign.

Activity: Launching and Optimising Your Facebook Ads Campaign

Now that you've learned the key concepts and strategies for creating successful Facebook Ads campaigns, it's time to put that knowledge into action. This activity will guide you through the process of launching and optimising your campaign.

1. **Define Your Campaign Objective:**
   - Choose an objective that aligns with your business goals, such as driving traffic, generating leads, or increasing conversions.
2. **Set Up Your Ad Set:**

- Define your target audience, budget, schedule, and ad placements. Use Facebook's Audience Insights tool to refine your audience targeting.
3. **Create Your Ad Content:**
   - Craft compelling ad copy, choose engaging visuals, and include a strong call-to-action. Test different ad formats to see which performs best.
4. **Install Facebook Pixel:**
   - If you haven't already, install the Facebook Pixel on your website to track user interactions and measure conversions. Use the data to optimise your campaigns.
5. **Launch Your Campaign:**
   - Once your campaign is set up, launch it and start monitoring its performance. Use Facebook Ads Manager to track key metrics and make data-driven adjustments.
6. **Optimise Your Campaign:**
   - Conduct A/B tests to refine your ad copy, creative, and audience targeting. Reallocate your budget to focus on high-performing ad sets and use ad scheduling to reach your audience at the right times.
7. **Measure Success:**
   - Track your campaign's success using key metrics such as CTR, conversions, and ROAS. Use the insights gained to continuously optimise your campaign and improve results.

By completing this activity, you'll be well on your way to mastering Facebook Ads and creating campaigns that drive meaningful business growth. Remember, the key to success with Facebook Ads is continuous optimisation and a willingness to experiment with different strategies.

Looking Ahead

With a solid understanding of Facebook Ads under your belt, it's time to explore another powerful platform: Instagram Ads. In the next chapter, we'll dive into the world of Instagram advertising, where you'll learn how to create visually compelling ads, reach your target audience, and build brand awareness on one of the most popular social media platforms.

As with Facebook Ads, success on Instagram requires a strategic approach, creative content, and ongoing optimisation. By mastering both platforms, you can create a comprehensive social media marketing strategy that drives results for your business.

Chapter 7: Mastering Instagram Ads for Visual Impact and Engagement

Introduction

Instagram has evolved from a simple photo-sharing app into a powerful platform for businesses to connect with their audience in visually compelling ways. With over 1 billion monthly active users, Instagram offers unparalleled opportunities for brands to showcase their products, tell their stories, and engage with a diverse audience. For franchisees and franchisors, Instagram Ads can be a critical component of a successful digital marketing strategy, especially if your brand relies on strong visuals to attract and retain customers.

In this chapter, we'll explore the ins and outs of Instagram Ads, from setting up your first campaign to advanced targeting strategies and creative best practices. We'll also discuss how to measure the success of your campaigns and continuously optimise them for better results. By the end of this chapter, you'll have the knowledge and confidence to create Instagram Ads that drive engagement, build brand awareness, and contribute to your business's growth.

Understanding the Instagram Ads Platform

Before diving into campaign creation, it's important to understand the unique features of the Instagram Ads platform and how it integrates with Facebook Ads Manager. Since Instagram is owned by Facebook, the process of creating and managing Instagram Ads is closely tied to the Facebook Ads platform.

1. The Integration with Facebook Ads Manager

Instagram Ads are created and managed through Facebook Ads Manager, which means that the process of setting up campaigns, defining audiences, and tracking performance is nearly identical to that of Facebook Ads. This integration allows you to run campaigns across both platforms simultaneously, making it easier to manage your social media advertising efforts in one place.

- **Shared Tools:** You can use the same tools for audience targeting, ad creation, and performance measurement across both Facebook and Instagram. This includes Custom Audiences, Lookalike Audiences, and the Facebook Pixel.
- **Cross-Platform Campaigns:** Running campaigns on both Facebook and Instagram can help you reach a broader audience and reinforce your messaging across multiple touchpoints. You can choose to run the same ads on both platforms or create platform-specific content.

2. Ad Formats on Instagram

Instagram offers a variety of ad formats designed to help you achieve different marketing objectives. Understanding these formats and when to use them is key to creating effective Instagram Ads.

- **Photo Ads:** These are single image ads that appear in users' Instagram feeds. Photo ads are simple yet powerful, especially if you have high-quality images that can grab users' attention as they scroll.
  - o **Example:** A franchisee of a beauty salon might use a photo ad featuring a close-up of a customer enjoying a relaxing facial treatment, with a call-to-action to book an appointment.
- **Video Ads:** Video ads can be up to 60 seconds long and appear in users' feeds or Stories. Videos

are great for showcasing products in action, telling a story, or demonstrating how your business operates.

- o **Example:** A franchisor of a fast-casual restaurant chain might use a video ad to show the process of preparing a signature dish, highlighting the freshness of the ingredients and the care taken in its preparation.
- **Carousel Ads:** Carousel ads allow you to showcase multiple images or videos within a single ad, which users can swipe through. This format is ideal for showing off a variety of products or telling a multi-part story.
  - o **Example:** A franchisee of a clothing boutique might use a carousel ad to display different outfits from their latest collection, with each slide featuring a different ensemble.
- **Story Ads:** Story ads appear between users' Instagram Stories and can be either photos or videos. These full-screen ads are immersive and can be particularly effective for driving engagement.
  - o **Example:** A franchisor of a fitness brand might use a Story ad to promote a limited-time offer on gym memberships, with a swipe-up link to sign up.
- **Collection Ads:** Collection ads combine a video or image with a product catalogue, allowing users to discover and purchase products directly from the ad. This format is ideal for e-commerce businesses.
  - o **Example:** A franchisee of an online home decor store might use a collection ad to showcase a video of a beautifully decorated living room, with product tiles below featuring the items used in the setup.

- **Explore Ads:** These ads appear in the Explore tab, where users discover new content and accounts. Explore ads can help you reach users who are actively looking for new things to engage with.
  - **Example:** A franchisee of a travel agency might use an Explore ad to promote exotic vacation packages, targeting users who are exploring travel-related content.

Case Study: Choosing the Right Ad Format

A franchisee of a luxury spa wanted to increase bookings for their signature massage treatment. They decided to use a combination of photo ads and Story ads to promote the offer.

- **Photo Ad:** The franchisee used a high-quality image of a relaxing spa environment with a call-to-action to book the massage online. The ad ran in users' feeds, targeting individuals interested in wellness and self-care.
- **Story Ad:** The franchisee created a 15-second video Story ad showing a customer enjoying the massage, with a swipe-up link to book the treatment. The ad was targeted to users who had recently engaged with similar wellness content on Instagram.

The combination of photo and Story ads resulted in a 25% increase in bookings for the signature massage treatment, demonstrating the effectiveness of using multiple ad formats to reach and engage the target audience.

Setting Up Your First Instagram Ads Campaign

Now that you understand the basics of Instagram Ads, it's time to set up your first campaign. This section will guide you through the process, from defining your objectives to creating compelling ad content.

1. Define Your Campaign Objective

As with Facebook Ads, the first step in creating an Instagram Ads campaign is to define your objective. Your objective should align with your business goals, whether that's increasing brand awareness, driving traffic to your website, or boosting sales.

- **Example:** A franchisee of a local coffee shop wants to attract more customers to their new location. They choose the "Store Traffic" objective to drive foot traffic to the shop.

2. Set Up Your Ad Set

Once you've defined your objective, the next step is to set up your ad set. This involves defining your target audience, budget, schedule, and placements.

- **Audience Targeting:** Use Instagram's audience targeting options to define who you want to reach. You can target users based on demographics, interests, behaviours, and more.
  - **Example:** The coffee shop franchisee targets users aged 18-35 within a 3-mile radius of the shop, who are interested in coffee, food, and local businesses.
- **Budget and Schedule:** Set your daily or lifetime budget and determine how long you want your ads to run. You can schedule your ads to run at specific times or continuously throughout the day.

- ○ **Example:** The franchisee sets a daily budget of £30 and schedules the ads to run during the morning and afternoon, when people are most likely to be looking for coffee.
- **Placements:** Since you're focusing on Instagram, select Instagram-specific placements, such as Instagram Feed, Stories, and Explore. You can also choose automatic placements to allow Instagram to optimise your ad delivery.
  - ○ **Example:** The franchisee selects Instagram Feed and Stories as the placements for their ads, ensuring they reach users in both browsing and immersive environments.

3. Create Your Ad Content

With your ad set defined, it's time to create the ad content itself. This involves crafting engaging ad copy, choosing eye-catching visuals, and including a strong call-to-action.

- **Ad Format:** Choose the format that best suits your campaign objectives, such as photo, video, or carousel ads.
  - ○ **Example:** The coffee shop franchisee chooses a carousel ad format to showcase multiple images of the new shop's interior, specialty drinks, and pastries.
- **Ad Copy:** Write clear and compelling ad copy that conveys your message and encourages users to take action. Focus on what makes your offer unique and why users should care.
  - ○ **Example:** The ad copy reads: "Discover our new coffee shop in [City Name]! Enjoy handcrafted lattes, fresh pastries, and a cosy atmosphere. Visit us today!"

- **Call-to-Action (CTA):** Include a CTA that directs users to take the next step, such as "Learn More," "Visit Us," or "Shop Now."
  - **Example:** The CTA button reads "Visit Us," directing users to a landing page with the shop's address, hours, and a map.

Case Study: Creating Engaging Ad Content

A franchisee of a high-end fashion boutique wanted to promote their seasonal sale on Instagram. They used a combination of video and carousel ads to showcase the sale items and encourage users to visit the boutique.

- **Video Ad:** The franchisee created a 30-second video ad featuring models wearing the boutique's top sale items. The video included dynamic transitions between outfits and a CTA to "Shop the Sale Now."
- **Carousel Ad:** The franchisee also created a carousel ad with multiple images of the sale items, each with a brief description and price. The CTA button read "Shop Now," directing users to the boutique's website.

The combination of video and carousel ads resulted in a 40% increase in website traffic and a significant boost in in-store visits during the sale period. The visually engaging content and clear messaging helped drive interest and conversions.

Advanced Targeting Strategies on Instagram

To get the most out of your Instagram Ads, it's important to go beyond basic targeting and explore more advanced strategies. These strategies can help you reach a highly relevant audience and maximise the impact of your campaigns.

1. Custom Audiences on Instagram

Custom Audiences allow you to target users who have already interacted with your business, whether through your website, Instagram profile, or customer list. This is a powerful way to re-engage existing customers or users who are familiar with your brand.

- **Website Custom Audiences:** Use the Facebook Pixel to create audiences based on users who have visited specific pages on your website or taken certain actions, such as adding items to their cart but not completing the purchase.
  - **Example:** A franchisee of an online beauty store creates a Custom Audience of users who browsed the skincare section but didn't make a purchase. They then retarget these users with an Instagram ad offering a discount on skincare products.
- **Engagement Custom Audiences:** Target users who have interacted with your Instagram profile, such as liking a post, watching a video, or clicking on an ad.
  - **Example:** A franchisor of a national restaurant chain creates a Custom Audience of users who engaged with a recent post promoting a new menu item. They then target these users with an ad offering a special deal on the item.

2. Lookalike Audiences on Instagram

Lookalike Audiences allow you to reach new users who are similar to your existing customers. By using data from your Custom Audiences, Instagram identifies users who share similar characteristics and behaviours, making them more likely to be interested in your business.

- **Creating Lookalike Audiences:** Start with a source audience, such as a list of your best customers or users who have made a purchase on your website. Instagram then finds users who closely match the characteristics of this audience.
  - ○ **Example:** A franchisee of a luxury home decor brand creates a Lookalike Audience based on their top customers, targeting users who are likely to be interested in high-end home furnishings.
- **Refining Lookalike Audiences:** You can adjust the percentage of similarity when creating a Lookalike Audience. A 1% Lookalike Audience closely matches your source audience, while a 5% Lookalike Audience is broader but less precise.
  - ○ **Example:** A franchisee of a fitness apparel brand creates a 2% Lookalike Audience to target users who share similar interests and behaviours with their most loyal customers, focusing on promoting a new activewear collection.

3. Detailed Interest Targeting on Instagram

Detailed interest targeting allows you to target users based on their specific interests, activities, and behaviours. This can help you reach a highly specific audience that aligns with your business's products or services.

- **Interest Categories:** Instagram offers a wide range of interest categories, such as fashion, fitness, travel, and more. You can select multiple interests to narrow down your audience.
  - ○ **Example:** A franchisee of a travel agency targets users interested in "adventure travel," "luxury resorts," and "beach

vacations" to promote their latest vacation packages.

- **Behavioural Targeting:** In addition to interests, you can target users based on their online and offline behaviours, such as purchasing habits, device usage, and travel patterns.
  - ○ **Example:** A franchisor of an e-commerce brand targets users who have made online purchases in the past 30 days, promoting a limited-time sale event.

Case Study: Advanced Targeting for Maximum Impact

A franchisee of a high-end jewellery store wanted to increase sales during the holiday season. They used a combination of Custom Audiences, Lookalike Audiences, and detailed interest targeting to reach a highly relevant audience on Instagram.

- **Custom Audience:** The franchisee created a Custom Audience of users who had visited their website's product pages but hadn't completed a purchase. They retargeted these users with ads promoting holiday discounts on luxury jewellery.
- **Lookalike Audience:** They also created a 1% Lookalike Audience based on their top customers, targeting users who were likely to be interested in high-end jewellery.
- **Interest Targeting:** To further refine their audience, the franchisee targeted users interested in "luxury goods," "fashion," and "gifts for her."

The advanced targeting strategy resulted in a 50% increase in online sales and a 30% increase in in-store visits during the holiday season. The combination of retargeting, Lookalike Audiences, and interest targeting helped the franchisee reach a highly engaged audience and maximise their campaign's effectiveness.

Measuring Success and Optimising Instagram Ads Campaigns

Creating and launching an Instagram Ads campaign is just the beginning. To ensure your campaigns are delivering the desired results, it's essential to monitor performance, measure success, and continuously optimise your ads.

1. Key Metrics to Track on Instagram

Instagram provides a range of metrics to help you track the performance of your ads. Here are some key metrics to monitor:

- **Reach:** The number of unique users who saw your ad. A higher reach indicates that your ad is being shown to a large audience.
- **Impressions:** The total number of times your ad was shown. Multiple impressions can occur when a user sees your ad more than once.
- **Engagement Rate:** The percentage of users who interacted with your ad, such as liking, commenting, or sharing. A higher engagement rate suggests that your ad is resonating with your audience.
- **Click-Through Rate (CTR):** The percentage of users who clicked on your ad after seeing it. A higher CTR indicates that your ad is compelling and relevant to your audience.
- **Conversions:** The number of desired actions taken by users, such as making a purchase, signing up for a newsletter, or downloading an app. Conversions are the ultimate measure of your campaign's success.
- **Return on Ad Spend (ROAS):** The revenue generated from your ad campaign divided by the cost of the campaign. A higher ROAS

indicates that your campaign is delivering a strong return on investment.

2. A/B Testing and Experimentation on Instagram

A/B testing, also known as split testing, is a powerful method for optimising your Instagram Ads campaigns. By testing different versions of your ads, you can determine which elements are most effective and make data-driven decisions to improve performance.

- **Ad Creative:** Test different images, videos, and ad formats to see which visuals resonate most with your audience.
  - o **Example:** A franchisee of a luxury spa tests a single image ad against a video ad showcasing a relaxation treatment. The video ad outperforms the image ad, leading the franchisee to focus more on video content in future campaigns.
- **Ad Copy:** Experiment with different headlines, body text, and calls-to-action to see which combination generates the highest engagement and conversions.
  - o **Example:** A franchisor of a gourmet food brand tests two different CTAs: "Shop Now" vs. "Discover Our Collection." The test reveals that "Shop Now" generates a higher CTR, prompting the franchisor to use that CTA in future ads.
- **Audience Segments:** Test different audience segments, such as age groups, interests, or behaviours, to identify the most responsive demographic.
  - o **Example:** A franchisee of a fitness apparel brand tests ads targeting users interested in "running" vs. those interested in "yoga." The test shows that the yoga audience has a higher engagement rate, leading

the franchisee to create more yoga-focused content.

3. Budget and Bid Optimisation on Instagram

Optimising your budget and bids is crucial for maximising the effectiveness of your Instagram Ads campaigns. Here are some strategies to consider:

- **Budget Allocation:** Allocate more budget to high-performing ad sets and reduce or pause low-performing ones. Use Instagram's reporting tools to identify which ad sets are delivering the best results.
    - **Example:** A franchisee of a pet grooming service notices that ads targeting cat owners are performing better than those targeting dog owners. They allocate more budget to the cat owner audience to maximise conversions.
- **Bid Strategies:** Experiment with different bid strategies, such as lowest cost, cost cap, or bid cap, to find the one that delivers the best results for your campaign objectives.
    - **Example:** A franchisor of a national retail chain tests a cost cap strategy to control the maximum amount they're willing to pay for conversions. This strategy helps them stay within their budget while achieving a higher ROAS.
- **Ad Scheduling:** Use Instagram's ad scheduling feature to show your ads at times when your audience is most active and likely to convert. This can help reduce wasted spend and improve performance.
    - **Example:** A franchisee of a coffee shop schedules their ads to run in the early morning and late afternoon, when people are most likely to be thinking about

coffee. This targeted scheduling results in a higher CTR and more in-store visits.

Case Study: Continuous Optimisation for Better Results

A franchisee of a home cleaning service wanted to improve the performance of their Instagram Ads campaign. By implementing A/B testing, budget optimisation, and ad scheduling, they were able to achieve significant improvements.

- **A/B Testing:** The franchisee tested different ad creatives, including a before-and-after image of a cleaned room vs. a video showcasing the cleaning process. The video ad generated a 25% higher CTR, so they shifted their focus to video content.
- **Budget Optimisation:** The franchisee reallocated their budget to focus on the best-performing ad sets, which targeted working professionals and parents with young children. This resulted in a 30% increase in conversions.
- **Ad Scheduling:** By scheduling ads to run during the evening hours, when their target audience was most likely to be at home and thinking about cleaning services, the franchisee achieved a 20% reduction in CPC and a higher conversion rate.

Through continuous optimisation, the franchisee was able to double their ROAS and significantly increase the effectiveness of their Instagram Ads campaign.

Activity: Launching and Optimising Your Instagram Ads Campaign

Now that you've learned the key concepts and strategies for creating successful Instagram Ads campaigns, it's time to put that knowledge into action. This activity will guide you through the process of launching and optimising your campaign.

1. **Define Your Campaign Objective:**
   - Choose an objective that aligns with your business goals, such as driving traffic, generating leads, or increasing conversions.
2. **Set Up Your Ad Set:**
   - Define your target audience, budget, schedule, and ad placements. Use Instagram's audience targeting options to refine your audience.
3. **Create Your Ad Content:**
   - Craft engaging ad copy, choose eye-catching visuals, and include a strong call-to-action. Test different ad formats to see which performs best.
4. **Install Facebook Pixel:**
   - If you haven't already, install the Facebook Pixel on your website to track user interactions and measure conversions. Use the data to optimise your campaigns.
5. **Launch Your Campaign:**
   - Once your campaign is set up, launch it and start monitoring its performance. Use Instagram's reporting tools to track key metrics and make data-driven adjustments.
6. **Optimise Your Campaign:**
   - Conduct A/B tests to refine your ad copy, creative, and audience targeting. Reallocate your budget to focus on high-performing ad sets and use ad scheduling to reach your audience at the right times.
7. **Measure Success:**
   - Track your campaign's success using key metrics such as CTR, conversions, and ROAS. Use the insights gained to

continuously optimise your campaign and improve results.

By completing this activity, you'll be well on your way to mastering Instagram Ads and creating campaigns that drive meaningful business growth. Remember, the key to success with Instagram Ads is continuous optimisation and a willingness to experiment with different strategies.

Looking Ahead

With a solid understanding of Instagram Ads, you're now equipped to leverage this visually driven platform to its fullest potential. In the next chapter, we'll explore how to create a cohesive digital marketing strategy that integrates Google Ads, Google Business Profiles, Facebook Ads, and Instagram Ads. By unifying your efforts across these platforms, you can create a powerful and consistent brand presence that drives results for your business.

As you continue to refine your skills in digital advertising, remember that each platform offers unique opportunities and challenges. By mastering each platform and integrating them into a cohesive strategy, you'll be able to reach your audience more effectively and achieve your business goals.

Chapter 8: Integrating Your Digital Marketing Strategy

Introduction

Now that you've mastered the individual platforms—Google Ads, Google Business Profiles, Facebook Ads, and Instagram Ads—it's time to bring everything together into a cohesive digital marketing strategy. Integrating your efforts across these platforms can help you create a consistent brand presence, reach your target audience more effectively, and maximise your return on investment (ROI). For franchisees and franchisors, a unified strategy ensures that both national and local marketing efforts are aligned and working towards common goals.

In this chapter, we'll explore how to develop an integrated digital marketing strategy that leverages the strengths of each platform. We'll discuss how to coordinate campaigns, maintain brand consistency, and use data to optimise your overall strategy. By the end of this chapter, you'll have the tools and knowledge to create a powerful, unified approach to digital marketing that drives results across all channels.

The Benefits of an Integrated Marketing Strategy

Before diving into the specifics of how to integrate your digital marketing efforts, it's important to understand the benefits of doing so. A well-integrated strategy offers several key advantages:

1. Consistent Brand Messaging

One of the most significant benefits of an integrated marketing strategy is the ability to maintain consistent brand messaging across all platforms. Whether a customer interacts with your brand on Google, Facebook, Instagram, or through your website, they should experience a unified and cohesive brand message.

- **Example:** A franchisor of a fast-casual dining chain ensures that all digital marketing materials, from Google Ads to Instagram posts, use the same brand colours, logos, and tone of voice. This consistency helps reinforce the brand's identity and makes it more recognisable to customers.

2. Improved Customer Experience

When your digital marketing efforts are integrated, you can provide a seamless customer experience across all touchpoints. This means that customers receive the same high-quality experience whether they're searching for your business on Google, engaging with your social media content, or visiting your physical location.

- **Example:** A franchisee of a fitness centre creates an integrated campaign that starts with a Google Ad promoting a free trial, followed by retargeting ads on Facebook and Instagram that remind users to sign up. When customers visit the gym, they find that the messaging and offers they saw online are mirrored in the in-person experience, creating a seamless journey.

3. Efficient Use of Resources

By coordinating your marketing efforts across platforms, you can make more efficient use of your resources, both in terms of budget and time. Instead of running separate campaigns with different objectives, you can align your goals and ensure that all your marketing activities are working towards the same outcomes.

- **Example:** A franchisor of a retail brand coordinates their Google Ads, Facebook Ads, and Instagram Ads to all promote a seasonal sale. By using similar creatives and targeting strategies across platforms, they maximise their reach while keeping their messaging consistent.

4. Enhanced Data and Insights

An integrated strategy allows you to gather data from multiple platforms and use it to gain a comprehensive understanding of your customers and campaign performance. This holistic view enables you to make more informed decisions and optimise your marketing efforts across the board.

- **Example:** A franchisee of an e-commerce store tracks customer behaviour across Google Ads, Facebook, and Instagram, using data from the Facebook Pixel and Google Analytics. They analyse the data to identify which platforms are driving the most conversions and adjust their strategy accordingly.

Developing Your Integrated Digital Marketing Strategy

Creating an integrated digital marketing strategy involves several key steps. Here's how to develop a strategy that leverages the strengths of each platform while ensuring that all efforts are aligned and working towards common goals.

1. Define Your Goals and Objectives

The first step in developing an integrated strategy is to define your overall goals and objectives. These should align with your business's broader goals, whether that's increasing brand awareness, driving sales, or growing your customer base. Your objectives should be specific, measurable, achievable, relevant, and time-bound (SMART).

- **Example:** A franchisor of a home services brand sets a goal to increase online bookings by 25% over the next six months. To achieve this, they create a digital marketing strategy that integrates Google Ads, Google Business Profiles, Facebook Ads, and Instagram Ads, all working together to drive traffic to their booking page.

2. Understand Your Audience

To create an effective integrated strategy, you need to have a deep understanding of your target audience. This includes knowing their demographics, interests, behaviours, and preferences. Use the insights gained from each platform's analytics tools, such as Google Analytics, Facebook Audience Insights, and Instagram Insights, to build a comprehensive profile of your audience.

- **Example:** A franchisee of a children's educational franchise identifies that their target audience consists of parents aged 25-45 who are interested in early childhood education, parenting tips, and local community events. They use this information to create targeted campaigns across Google, Facebook, and Instagram.

3. Align Your Messaging and Creative

Once you have a clear understanding of your goals and audience, the next step is to align your messaging and creative across all platforms. This means ensuring that your brand's voice, tone, and visual identity are consistent, whether customers encounter your brand on Google, Facebook, or Instagram.

- **Example:** A franchisor of a luxury hotel chain develops a unified creative concept for their new marketing campaign. The concept includes high-quality visuals of their properties, a consistent colour palette, and messaging that highlights the unique experiences offered at each location. This creative is adapted for use across Google Ads, Facebook Ads, and Instagram Ads, ensuring that the brand's message is consistent everywhere.

4. Coordinate Campaigns Across Platforms

To maximise the impact of your integrated strategy, coordinate your campaigns across all platforms. This means planning your campaigns so that they support each other and work together to achieve your objectives. For example, you might use Google Ads to drive traffic to your website, where users can sign up for a newsletter that you promote on Facebook and Instagram.

- **Example:** A franchisee of a local bakery launches a campaign to promote a new line of gourmet cupcakes. They start with a Google Ads campaign to drive traffic to a landing page, where customers can sign up for a discount. They then retarget those users with Facebook and Instagram ads reminding them to redeem the discount in-store.

5. Use Data to Drive Decision-Making

An integrated strategy requires a data-driven approach to decision-making. Use the analytics tools available on each platform to track your campaign performance, measure success, and identify areas for improvement.

Regularly review your data to see which platforms and tactics are delivering the best results and adjust your strategy accordingly.

- **Example:** A franchisor of a national fitness chain monitors the performance of their integrated campaign using Google Analytics, Facebook Ads Manager, and Instagram Insights. They discover that Instagram Stories ads are driving the most engagement and conversions, so they allocate more budget to that format while scaling back on less effective tactics.

Case Study: Implementing an Integrated Strategy

A franchisee of a high-end spa wanted to increase bookings for their new treatment package. They developed an integrated digital marketing strategy that leveraged Google Ads, Google Business Profiles, Facebook Ads, and Instagram Ads.

- **Goal:** Increase bookings for the new treatment package by 30% over three months.
- **Audience:** The franchisee targeted women aged 30-55 who were interested in wellness, luxury experiences, and self-care.
- **Messaging and Creative:** The campaign featured luxurious images of the spa and the treatment, with messaging focused on relaxation and rejuvenation. The same creative was adapted for use across all platforms.
- **Campaign Coordination:** The franchisee used Google Ads to drive traffic to a landing page where users could learn more about the treatment and book online. They retargeted users who visited the page with Facebook and Instagram ads that featured customer testimonials, and a limited time offer.

- **Data-Driven Decisions:** Throughout the campaign, the franchisee monitored performance using data from Google Analytics, Facebook Ads Manager, and Instagram Insights. They identified that Instagram Stories were particularly effective, so they increased the budget for that placement.

The integrated strategy resulted in a 35% increase in bookings for the new treatment package, exceeding the franchisee's goal. The consistent messaging and coordinated efforts across all platforms helped create a seamless customer experience that drove conversions.

Optimising Your Integrated Strategy

Once your integrated digital marketing strategy is in place, it's important to continuously optimise it to ensure that you're getting the best possible results. Here are some tips for ongoing optimisation:

1. Regularly Review and Adjust Campaigns

Digital marketing is dynamic, and what works today might not work tomorrow. Regularly review your campaign performance across all platforms and be prepared to adjust as needed. This might involve tweaking your messaging, changing your ad creatives, or reallocating your budget to more effective tactics.

- **Example:** A franchisor of a national retail brand reviews their campaign data every two weeks. They notice that engagement rates are declining on Facebook, so they test new ad creatives and adjust their targeting to re-engage their audience.

2. Leverage Cross-Platform Insights

The insights you gain from one platform can often be applied to others. For example, if you find that a particular audience segment is responding well to your Facebook Ads, consider targeting that same segment with your Google Ads or Instagram Ads. Cross-platform insights can help you refine your overall strategy and maximise your ROI.

- **Example:** A franchisee of an online pet supply store discovers that their Facebook Ads are performing well among pet owners who are interested in eco-friendly products. They use this insight to create a new Google Ads campaign targeting the same audience with keywords related to eco-friendly pet supplies.

3. Test and Experiment

Don't be afraid to experiment with new tactics, formats, and platforms as part of your integrated strategy. Testing different approaches can help you discover what resonates most with your audience and uncover new opportunities for growth.

- **Example:** A franchisee of a luxury travel agency decides to experiment with Instagram Explore ads to reach users who are actively searching for travel inspiration. They create a series of visually stunning ads featuring exotic destinations, and the experiment results in a 20% increase in website visits from Instagram.

4. Focus on the Customer Journey

An integrated strategy should always keep the customer journey in mind. Consider how each touchpoint— whether it's a Google search, a Facebook ad, or an Instagram post—fits into the broader customer journey and how you can create a seamless experience that guides users from awareness to conversion.

- **Example:** A franchisor of a home improvement brand maps out the customer journey from initial awareness to final purchase. They use Google Ads to capture users at the awareness stage, Facebook Ads to build interest, and Instagram Ads to drive conversions. The journey is seamless, with consistent messaging and a clear path to conversion.

Case Study: Optimising an Integrated Strategy

A franchisee of a gourmet food delivery service launched an integrated digital marketing strategy to increase subscriptions. Over time, they continuously optimised their strategy to improve results.

- **Regular Review:** The franchisee reviewed campaign data weekly, tracking key metrics like CTR, conversion rates, and ROAS. They identified that Facebook Ads were driving the most conversions, so they increased the budget for that platform.
- **Cross-Platform Insights:** They noticed that users who engaged with their Facebook Ads were also likely to engage with their Instagram content. They used this insight to create a cross-platform campaign that targeted the same audience with different creatives on each platform.
- **Testing and Experimentation:** The franchisee tested different ad formats, such as carousel ads on Instagram and video ads on Facebook. They found that video ads performed best, so they shifted their focus to creating more video content.
- **Customer Journey:** The franchisee focused on creating a seamless customer journey, starting

with awareness on Google, building interest on Facebook, and driving conversions on Instagram. They used consistent messaging and clear calls-to-action to guide users through the journey.

Through continuous optimisation, the franchisee was able to increase subscriptions by 50% over six months. The integrated strategy, combined with regular testing and a focus on the customer journey, helped them achieve their goals.

Activity: Creating Your Integrated Digital Marketing Strategy

Now that you've learned the key concepts and strategies for creating an integrated digital marketing strategy, it's time to put that knowledge into action. This activity will guide you through the process of developing and optimising your strategy.

1. **Define Your Goals and Objectives:**
   o Identify the specific goals you want to achieve with your digital marketing strategy. Ensure that your objectives are SMART and align with your broader business goals.
2. **Understand Your Audience:**
   o Use the analytics tools available on each platform to build a comprehensive profile of your target audience. Consider demographics, interests, behaviours, and preferences.
3. **Align Your Messaging and Creative:**
   o Develop a unified creative concept and messaging that can be adapted for use across all platforms. Ensure that your brand's voice, tone, and visual identity are consistent.
4. **Coordinate Campaigns Across Platforms:**

- o Plan and execute campaigns that support each other across Google Ads, Google Business Profiles, Facebook Ads, and Instagram Ads. Ensure that all efforts are aligned and working towards common goals.

5. **Use Data to Drive Decision-Making:**
   - o Regularly monitor your campaign performance using the analytics tools available on each platform. Use the data to make informed decisions and optimise your strategy.

6. **Optimise Your Strategy:**
   - o Continuously review and adjust your campaigns based on performance data. Leverage cross-platform insights, experiment with new tactics, and focus on creating a seamless customer journey.

7. **Measure Success:**
   - o Track your strategy's success using key metrics such as conversions, engagement rates, and ROAS. Use the insights gained to refine your strategy and achieve better results over time.

By completing this activity, you'll be well on your way to creating a powerful, integrated digital marketing strategy that drives meaningful business growth. Remember, the key to success is continuous optimisation and a willingness to adapt to changing circumstances.

Looking Ahead

With a comprehensive and integrated digital marketing strategy in place, you're now positioned to take full advantage of the opportunities offered by online platforms. In the final chapter, we'll explore how to measure the long-term success of your digital marketing efforts, how to stay ahead of industry trends, and how to ensure that your strategy continues to evolve as your business grows.

Digital marketing is an ongoing process, and the strategies you've learned in this book are just the beginning. By staying informed, embracing innovation, and continuously refining your approach, you can build a strong digital presence that supports your business's success for years to come.

Chapter 9: Measuring Long-Term Success and Adapting to Trends

Introduction

With your integrated digital marketing strategy in place, the next step is to ensure its long-term success. This involves not only measuring the effectiveness of your campaigns but also staying ahead of industry trends and continuously adapting your strategy to meet the evolving needs of your business. For franchisees and franchisors, understanding how to measure success over time and how to pivot when necessary is crucial for sustained growth and competitiveness in the market.

In this chapter, we'll explore the key metrics and tools you can use to measure the long-term success of your digital marketing efforts. We'll also discuss how to stay informed about emerging trends, how to anticipate changes in consumer behaviour, and how to ensure that your strategy remains flexible and adaptable. By the end of this chapter, you'll have a roadmap for maintaining the effectiveness of your digital marketing strategy over the long term.

Measuring Long-Term Success

Measuring the success of your digital marketing efforts is not just about looking at immediate results; it's about understanding how your campaigns contribute to your overall business goals over time. To do this, you need to focus on both short-term and long-term metrics and regularly review your performance to make data-driven decisions.

1. Key Performance Indicators (KPIs) for Long-Term Success

Key Performance Indicators (KPIs) are specific metrics that help you measure the effectiveness of your digital marketing strategy. While KPIs will vary depending on your business goals, some common long-term KPIs include:

- **Customer Lifetime Value (CLV):** This metric measures the total revenue that a customer is expected to generate for your business over their lifetime. Increasing CLV is a sign that your marketing efforts are not only attracting new customers but also retaining them and encouraging repeat purchases.
    - ○ **Example:** A franchisor of a subscription-based meal delivery service tracks CLV to measure the effectiveness of their retention strategies. By increasing the average subscription duration through targeted email campaigns and loyalty programs, they boost overall revenue.
- **Return on Investment (ROI):** ROI measures the profitability of your digital marketing campaigns relative to their cost. A positive ROI indicates that your campaigns are generating more revenue than they are costing.
    - ○ **Example:** A franchisee of a local fitness centre calculates the ROI of their digital marketing efforts by comparing the revenue generated from new memberships to the cost of their Google Ads and social media campaigns.
- **Customer Acquisition Cost (CAC):** CAC is the cost of acquiring a new customer through your marketing efforts. Lowering CAC while maintaining or increasing sales is a key indicator of an efficient marketing strategy.
    - ○ **Example:** A franchisor of a retail brand tracks CAC across different channels, such as Google Ads, Facebook Ads, and Instagram Ads, to identify which platform

offers the most cost-effective customer acquisition.

- **Brand Awareness:** While more difficult to quantify, brand awareness is a critical long-term metric that reflects how well-known and recognized your brand is within your target market. Surveys, social media engagement, and direct traffic to your website can all provide insights into brand awareness.
  - o **Example:** A franchisee of a boutique hotel chain uses social media mentions, branded search queries, and direct website traffic as indicators of growing brand awareness in their region.
- **Customer Retention Rate:** This metric measures the percentage of customers who continue to do business with you over time. A high retention rate suggests that your marketing and customer service efforts are successfully keeping customers engaged and satisfied.
  - o **Example:** A franchisor of a home cleaning service monitors customer retention rates by tracking repeat bookings and customer loyalty program participation.

2. Tools for Tracking Long-Term Success

To effectively measure and track your long-term KPIs, you'll need to leverage a variety of tools and platforms. Here are some of the most commonly used tools for monitoring digital marketing performance over time:

- **Google Analytics:** Google Analytics is a powerful tool for tracking website traffic, user behaviour, and conversions. It allows you to measure the effectiveness of your marketing campaigns and understand how users interact with your site.
  - o **Example:** A franchisee of an online education platform uses Google Analytics

to track the number of new student sign-ups and their journey through the website, helping to identify opportunities for improving the user experience and increasing conversions.

- **Facebook Ads Manager:** Facebook Ads Manager provides detailed insights into the performance of your Facebook and Instagram campaigns, including reach, engagement, conversions, and ROAS. It also allows you to track Custom Audiences and retargeting efforts.
  - ○ **Example:** A franchisee of a beauty salon uses Facebook Ads Manager to monitor the success of their Instagram Ads campaign, tracking the number of bookings generated and the cost per acquisition.
- **CRM Systems:** Customer Relationship Management [CRM] systems help you manage customer interactions, track sales, and monitor customer retention over time. They are essential for measuring long-term KPIs such as CLV and retention rate.
  - ○ **Example:** A franchisor of a national retail chain uses a CRM system to track customer purchase history, loyalty program participation, and overall customer satisfaction, allowing them to tailor marketing efforts and improve retention.
- **Survey Tools:** Tools like SurveyMonkey or Google Forms can be used to gather customer feedback and measure brand awareness, customer satisfaction, and overall experience. Regular surveys can provide valuable insights into how your brand is perceived over time.
  - ○ **Example:** A franchisee of a local restaurant chain regularly surveys customers to gauge satisfaction with the dining experience and gather feedback

on menu offerings. This data is used to make improvements and tailor marketing campaigns to customer preferences.

- **Social Media Analytics:** Each social media platform provides its own analytics tools, such as Instagram Insights and Twitter Analytics, which can help you track engagement, follower growth, and brand sentiment over time.
  - ○ **Example:** A franchisee of a fitness brand monitors Instagram Insights to track the growth of their follower base, the engagement rate of their posts, and the effectiveness of their influencer partnerships.

Case Study: Tracking Long-Term Success

A franchisee of a luxury spa wanted to measure the long-term success of their digital marketing efforts, focusing on increasing customer retention and lifetime value. They implemented a strategy that involved tracking key KPIs over a 12-month period.

- **Tools Used:** The franchisee used Google Analytics to track website traffic and conversions, a CRM system to monitor customer retention and purchase history, and Facebook Ads Manager to track the performance of their social media campaigns.
- **KPIs Tracked:** The key KPIs included Customer Lifetime Value (CLV), Customer Retention Rate, and Return on Investment (ROI).
- **Results:** Over the 12-month period, the franchisee increased CLV by 20% and customer retention by 15%. They also achieved a positive ROI of 150% on their digital marketing campaigns, demonstrating the long-term success of their strategy.

By regularly monitoring these KPIs and making data-driven adjustments to their marketing efforts, the franchisee was able to achieve sustained growth and profitability.

Staying Ahead of Industry Trends

The digital marketing landscape is constantly evolving, with new trends, technologies, and consumer behaviours emerging all the time. To maintain the effectiveness of your strategy, it's essential to stay informed about these trends and be prepared to adapt your approach as needed.

1. Identifying Emerging Trends

Staying ahead of industry trends involves regularly monitoring the digital marketing landscape and identifying new opportunities for growth. Here are some ways to keep your finger on the pulse of the industry:

- **Follow Industry Publications:** Subscribe to digital marketing blogs, newsletters, and podcasts to stay informed about the latest trends and best practices. Some popular sources include HubSpot, Moz, and Social Media Examiner.
  - **Example:** A franchisee of a home decor brand follows industry blogs to stay updated on the latest trends in social media advertising, content marketing, and SEO. They use this information to experiment with new tactics and improve their digital marketing strategy.
- **Attend Conferences and Webinars:** Industry conferences and webinars are great opportunities to learn from experts, network with peers, and gain insights into emerging trends. Look for events focused on digital marketing, social media, and online advertising.

- o **Example:** A franchisor of a national restaurant chain attends an annual digital marketing conference to learn about the latest advancements in mobile advertising and customer experience optimization.
- **Join Online Communities:** Participate in online communities, such as LinkedIn groups or Reddit forums, where digital marketers share tips, discuss challenges, and exchange ideas. These communities can be valuable sources of real-time information and inspiration.
  - o **Example:** A franchisee of an online tutoring service joins a LinkedIn group focused on educational technology and digital marketing. They use the group to connect with other marketers and stay informed about trends in online learning and content marketing.
- **Monitor Competitors:** Keep an eye on what your competitors are doing in the digital space. This can provide insights into new tactics or strategies that you can adapt for your own business.
  - o **Example:** A franchisee of a fitness apparel brand regularly reviews the social media profiles and online ads of competing brands to identify new trends in influencer marketing and customer engagement.

2. Adapting to Changes in Consumer Behaviour

Consumer behaviour is constantly evolving, influenced by changes in technology, social trends, and economic factors. To stay competitive, your digital marketing strategy must be flexible enough to adapt to these changes.

- **Personalisation:** As consumers increasingly expect personalised experiences, it's important to tailor your marketing messages and offers to individual preferences. Use data from your CRM system, social media, and website analytics to create personalised campaigns.

- Example: A franchisee of a luxury travel agency uses customer data to send personalised email offers based on past travel preferences, such as luxury beach resorts or adventure tours.

- **Mobile-First Strategies:** With more consumers using mobile devices to browse the web and make purchases, your digital marketing strategy should prioritise mobile-friendly content and ads. Ensure that your website, emails, and social media posts are optimised for mobile.
  - Example: A franchisor of an e-commerce brand ensures that all their online ads, landing pages, and email campaigns are fully responsive and designed with mobile users in mind.

- **Voice Search Optimisation:** As the use of voice search continues to grow, it's important to optimise your content for voice queries. This involves using natural language and long-tail keywords that reflect how people speak rather than type.
  - Example: A franchisee of a local pet supply store optimises their Google My Business listing and website content to include voice search-friendly phrases like "Where can I find organic dog food near me?"

- **Social Commerce:** Social media platforms are increasingly becoming shopping destinations, with features like Instagram Shopping and Facebook Marketplace allowing users to browse and purchase products directly. Consider incorporating social commerce into your strategy.
  - Example: A franchisee of a fashion boutique uses Instagram Shopping to

showcase their latest collections, allowing followers to purchase items directly from their Instagram feed.

Case Study: Adapting to Emerging Trends

A franchisee of an online education platform noticed a growing trend in the demand for microlearning—short, focused learning sessions that can be completed quickly. They decided to adapt their digital marketing strategy to take advantage of this trend.

- **Trend Identification:** The franchisee identified the microlearning trend by following industry publications, participating in online communities, and monitoring competitor activity.
- **Strategy Adaptation:** They developed a series of microlearning modules and promoted them through targeted Google Ads, Facebook Ads, and Instagram Stories. The modules were designed to be easily digestible and mobile-friendly, catering to busy professionals.
- **Results:** The microlearning campaign resulted in a 40% increase in course sign-ups and a 25% boost in engagement on social media. By adapting to the emerging trend, the franchisee was able to tap into a new market segment and grow their business.

Ensuring Flexibility and Adaptability in Your Strategy

The digital marketing landscape is dynamic, and your strategy must be flexible enough to adapt to changing conditions. Here are some tips for ensuring that your strategy remains adaptable and resilient:

1. Regularly Review and Update Your Strategy

Your digital marketing strategy should not be a static document. Regularly review your strategy to ensure that it aligns with your current business goals, market conditions, and consumer behaviour. Be prepared to make adjustments as needed.

- **Example:** A franchisor of a national retail brand conducts quarterly reviews of their digital marketing strategy, assessing the effectiveness of each channel and making adjustments based on performance data and market trends.

2. Embrace Experimentation and Innovation

To stay ahead in the competitive digital landscape, it's important to embrace experimentation and be willing to try new tactics. Innovation often comes from taking calculated risks and learning from both successes and failures.

- **Example:** A franchisee of a luxury hotel chain experiments with augmented reality (AR) ads on Instagram, allowing users to virtually tour their hotel rooms before booking. The experiment leads to increased engagement and higher booking rates.

3. Stay Agile and Responsive

An agile marketing strategy allows you to quickly respond to changes in the market, customer behaviour, or external factors. This might involve shifting your focus to a different platform, adjusting your messaging, or reallocating your budget to more effective channels.

- **Example:** A franchisee of a local restaurant chain notices a sudden increase in demand for delivery services due to changing consumer behaviour.

They quickly shift their digital marketing focus to promote their delivery options through Google Ads and Facebook.

4. Build a Culture of Continuous Learning

Encourage a culture of continuous learning within your marketing team. Stay curious, seek out new knowledge, and be open to adopting new tools, technologies, and strategies that can enhance your digital marketing efforts.

- **Example:** A franchisor of a national fitness brand invests in ongoing training for their marketing team, providing access to industry certifications, webinars, and workshops. This commitment to continuous learning helps the team stay on top of emerging trends and best practices.

Case Study: Ensuring Flexibility and Adaptability

A franchisee of a high-end retail brand wanted to ensure that their digital marketing strategy remained flexible and adaptable to changing conditions. They implemented several practices to achieve this goal.

- **Strategy Reviews:** The franchisee conducted monthly strategy reviews, assessing the performance of their campaigns and making adjustments based on real-time data and market conditions.
- **Experimentation:** They embraced a culture of experimentation, testing new ad formats, platforms, and targeting strategies to discover what worked best for their audience.
- **Agility:** The franchisee maintained an agile approach, quickly pivoting their strategy in

response to external factors, such as seasonal changes or economic shifts.
- **Continuous Learning:** They invested in continuous learning, providing their marketing team with access to the latest industry training and resources.

Through these practices, the franchisee was able to maintain a flexible and adaptable digital marketing strategy that consistently delivered strong results, even in the face of changing market conditions.

Activity: Measuring Success and Adapting Your Strategy

Now that you've learned the key concepts and strategies for measuring long-term success and adapting to industry trends, it's time to put that knowledge into action. This activity will guide you through the process of reviewing and optimising your digital marketing strategy.

1. **Identify Key KPIs:**
   - Determine the key performance indicators (KPIs) that are most important for measuring the long-term success of your digital marketing efforts. These might include CLV, ROI, CAC, brand awareness, and customer retention rate.
2. **Select the Right Tools:**
   - Choose the tools and platforms you'll use to track your KPIs, such as Google Analytics, Facebook Ads Manager, CRM systems, and survey tools. Ensure that you have the necessary resources and expertise to use these tools effectively.
3. **Monitor Industry Trends:**
   - Regularly monitor industry trends by following digital marketing publications, attending conferences, joining online

communities, and monitoring competitors. Use this information to identify emerging opportunities and threats.

4. **Adapt to Consumer Behaviour:**
   - Stay informed about changes in consumer behaviour and be prepared to adapt your digital marketing strategy accordingly. This might involve personalisation, mobile-first strategies, voice search optimisation, or social commerce.

5. **Review and Update Your Strategy:**
   - Regularly review your digital marketing strategy to ensure that it remains aligned with your business goals and market conditions. Be open to making adjustments and embracing new tactics.

6. **Experiment and Innovate:**
   - Embrace a culture of experimentation and innovation. Test new ideas, learn from your successes and failures, and continuously seek out opportunities to improve your digital marketing efforts.

7. **Maintain Flexibility and Agility:**
   - Ensure that your strategy remains flexible and agile, allowing you to quickly respond to changes in the market or external factors. Build a culture of continuous learning to keep your team informed and adaptable.

By completing this activity, you'll be well on your way to maintaining a successful and adaptable digital marketing strategy that drives long-term growth for your business. Remember, the key to sustained success is a commitment to continuous improvement, learning, and innovation.

Looking Ahead

As we reach the conclusion of this book, it's important to remember that digital marketing is a journey, not a destination. The strategies and tactics you've learned are powerful tools that can help you achieve your business goals, but the digital landscape is constantly evolving. To stay competitive, you must remain proactive, curious, and willing to adapt to new challenges and opportunities.

In the final chapter, we'll recap the key takeaways from the book and provide a roadmap for your continued growth and success in digital marketing. We'll also discuss how to stay motivated, stay inspired, and continue driving results for your franchise or business in the years to come.

Chapter 10: The Roadmap to Continued Growth and Success

Introduction

As we conclude this journey through the world of digital marketing, it's essential to reflect on what you've learned and how you can apply these insights to continue growing and succeeding in the years to come. Digital marketing is not a one-time effort; it's an ongoing process that requires dedication, adaptability, and a willingness to innovate. Whether you're a franchisee or a franchisor, the strategies and tactics you've developed will serve as the foundation for your continued success.

In this final chapter, we'll recap the key takeaways from the book and provide a roadmap for your ongoing digital marketing efforts. We'll also discuss how to stay motivated, stay inspired, and ensure that your marketing strategy evolves alongside your business. By the end of this chapter, you'll have a clear vision for the future and the tools you need to achieve your goals.

Recap of Key Takeaways

Throughout this book, we've explored a wide range of digital marketing strategies and tactics tailored specifically for franchisees and franchisors. Let's recap some of the most important lessons:

1. The Importance of a Strong Digital Presence

Your digital presence is the cornerstone of your marketing efforts. It's where potential customers first encounter your brand and where existing customers return to engage with your business. Ensuring that your Google Business Profile is fully optimised, your website is user-friendly, and your social media profiles are active and engaging is critical for attracting and retaining customers.

- **Action Item:** Regularly audit your digital presence to ensure that all profiles, listings, and content are up to date and aligned with your brand's messaging and goals.

2. The Power of Targeted Advertising

Digital advertising platforms like Google Ads, Facebook Ads, and Instagram Ads offer unparalleled opportunities to reach specific audiences with tailored messages. By leveraging advanced targeting options, such as Custom Audiences, Lookalike Audiences, and detailed interest targeting, you can maximise the impact of your campaigns and drive conversions.

- **Action Item:** Continuously refine your audience targeting strategies based on performance data and insights. Experiment with different ad formats and messaging to discover what resonates most with your audience.

3. The Value of Integration and Consistency

An integrated digital marketing strategy ensures that your efforts across different platforms are aligned and working towards the same goals. Consistency in messaging, branding, and customer experience across Google, Facebook, Instagram, and your website helps reinforce your brand and builds trust with your audience.

- **Action Item:** Develop a unified creative concept and messaging strategy that can be adapted for use across all digital marketing platforms. Ensure that your brand's voice, tone, and visual identity are consistent.

4. The Importance of Data-Driven Decision Making

Data is at the heart of successful digital marketing. By regularly monitoring your campaign performance and using tools like Google Analytics, Facebook Ads Manager, and CRM systems, you can make informed decisions that drive better results. Continuous optimisation based on data insights is key to long-term success.

- **Action Item:** Set up regular reporting processes to track key performance indicators (KPIs) such as Customer Lifetime Value (CLV), Return on Investment (ROI), and Customer Acquisition Cost (CAC). Use this data to guide your strategy and make adjustments as needed.

5. The Need for Flexibility and Adaptability

The digital marketing landscape is constantly changing, and your strategy must be flexible enough to adapt to new trends, technologies, and consumer behaviours. Staying informed about emerging trends and being willing to experiment with new tactics will help you stay ahead of the competition.

- **Action Item:** Regularly review your digital marketing strategy and be prepared to make adjustments based on market conditions, consumer behaviour, and industry trends. Encourage a culture of continuous learning and innovation within your team.

Staying Motivated and Inspired

As you continue your digital marketing journey, it's important to stay motivated and inspired. The road to success is not always smooth, and there will be challenges along the way. Here are some tips for staying motivated and maintaining your passion for digital marketing:

1. Set Clear and Achievable Goals

Setting clear and achievable goals gives you a sense of direction and purpose. Break down your long-term objectives into smaller, manageable tasks, and celebrate your successes along the way.

- **Example:** A franchisee of a local bakery sets a goal to increase online orders by 20% over the next quarter. They break this goal down into weekly tasks, such as launching a new Google Ads campaign, optimising their website for mobile users, and promoting special offers on social media.

2. Keep Learning and Growing

The digital marketing industry is dynamic, and there's always something new to learn. Stay curious and keep up with the latest developments in the field. Attend webinars, read industry publications, and participate in online communities to expand your knowledge and skills.

- **Example:** A franchisor of a national retail brand subscribes to digital marketing newsletters, attends industry conferences, and takes online courses to stay informed about the latest trends and best practices.

3. Stay Connected with Your Audience

Your customers are at the heart of your business, and staying connected with them is essential for success.

Engage with your audience on social media, respond to their feedback, and listen to their needs. Building strong relationships with your customers will keep you motivated and help you create marketing campaigns that resonate.

- **Example:** A franchisee of a fitness centre regularly interacts with members on social media, responding to comments, sharing user-generated content, and running polls to gather feedback on new class offerings.

4. Embrace Creativity and Innovation

Digital marketing is as much an art as it is a science. Embrace your creativity and look for innovative ways to connect with your audience. Experiment with new formats, platforms, and messaging strategies to keep your campaigns fresh and engaging.

- **Example:** A franchisee of a luxury travel agency creates an interactive virtual tour of their most popular destinations, allowing potential customers to explore the locations from the comfort of their homes. This creative approach helps differentiate their brand and attract new clients.

5. Celebrate Your Achievements

It's important to take time to celebrate your achievements, no matter how small. Recognising your successes can boost morale, keep you motivated, and remind you of how far you've come.

- **Example:** A franchisor of a national restaurant chain celebrates the successful launch of a new digital marketing campaign by hosting a team lunch and sharing the campaign's achievements with the entire company.

Case Study: Staying Motivated and Inspired

A franchisee of a high-end spa faced challenges in maintaining their digital marketing momentum after a series of successful campaigns. To stay motivated and inspired, they implemented several strategies:

- **Goal Setting:** They set new, ambitious goals for the next quarter, such as launching a loyalty program and increasing social media engagement by 30%.
- **Continuous Learning:** The franchisee enrolled in an advanced digital marketing course and attended industry webinars to stay informed about the latest trends.
- **Customer Engagement:** They focused on deepening their connection with customers by hosting virtual wellness events and sharing customer success stories on social media.
- **Creativity:** The franchisee experimented with new content formats, such as behind-the-scenes videos and influencer partnerships, to keep their campaigns fresh.
- **Celebrating Success:** They celebrated each milestone, such as reaching 10,000 followers on Instagram, by rewarding their team and sharing the achievement with their customers.

By staying motivated and inspired, the franchisee was able to maintain their digital marketing momentum and continue achieving their business goals.

Your Roadmap to Continued Growth and Success

As you move forward, it's important to have a clear roadmap for continued growth and success. Here's a step-by-step guide to help you stay on track:

1. Regularly Review and Update Your Strategy

Your digital marketing strategy should be a living document that evolves alongside your business. Schedule regular reviews to assess your performance, identify areas for improvement, and make necessary adjustments.

- **Action Item:** Set a quarterly review schedule to evaluate your digital marketing strategy, track KPIs, and make data-driven decisions.

2. Stay Informed About Industry Trends

The digital marketing landscape is constantly changing, and staying informed about emerging trends is essential for maintaining your competitive edge. Dedicate time each week to read industry publications, attend webinars, and participate in online communities.

- **Action Item:** Subscribe to digital marketing newsletters, join relevant LinkedIn groups, and attend at least one industry conference or webinar each quarter.

3. Foster a Culture of Continuous Learning

Encourage a culture of continuous learning within your team. Provide opportunities for professional development, such as training courses, certifications, and workshops. Staying informed and up-to-date will help you stay ahead of the competition.

- **Action Item:** Allocate a portion of your budget for ongoing training and development. Encourage team members to pursue certifications in areas such as Google Ads, Facebook Blueprint, and SEO.

4. Embrace Innovation and Experimentation

Innovation is key to staying relevant in the digital marketing world. Don't be afraid to experiment with new tactics, platforms, and creative approaches. Learning from both successes and failures will help you refine your strategy and achieve better results.

- **Action Item:** Set aside time and budget for experimentation. Test new ad formats, try out emerging platforms, and explore creative content ideas.

5. Stay Connected with Your Audience

Your customers are your most valuable asset. Stay connected with them by engaging on social media, responding to feedback, and offering personalised experiences. Building strong relationships with your audience will drive loyalty and long-term success.

- **Action Item:** Create a customer engagement plan that includes regular social media interaction, surveys, and personalised marketing campaigns.

6. Measure Success and Adapt as Needed

Regularly track your KPIs and use data to guide your decision-making. Be prepared to adapt your strategy based on performance data, market conditions, and changing consumer behaviour.

- **Action Item:** Set up automated reports to track your KPIs and schedule monthly meetings to review performance and make strategic adjustments.

Case Study: A Roadmap to Success

A franchisee of a national retail chain used a structured roadmap to guide their digital marketing efforts over a two-year period. By following the steps outlined above, they achieved significant growth and success:

- **Strategy Review:** They conducted quarterly strategy reviews, making adjustments based on performance data and market trends.
- **Industry Trends:** They stayed informed about emerging trends, such as the rise of social commerce and the importance of mobile-first strategies.
- **Continuous Learning:** The franchisee and their team pursued certifications in Google Ads and social media marketing, enhancing their skills and knowledge.
- **Innovation:** They experimented with new content formats, such as interactive videos and AR ads, which helped differentiate their brand and attract new customers.
- **Customer Engagement:** They deepened their connection with customers by launching a loyalty program and hosting online events.
- **Success Measurement:** They regularly tracked their KPIs, achieving a 40% increase in online sales and a 30% boost in customer retention over two years.

By following this roadmap, the franchisee was able to achieve sustained growth and success in their digital marketing efforts.

Conclusion: Your Journey Ahead

As you embark on the next phase of your digital marketing journey, remember that success is not a destination but an ongoing process. The strategies, tactics, and insights you've gained from this book are powerful tools that will help you navigate the ever-changing digital landscape. But your journey doesn't end here—it's just beginning.

Stay motivated, stay informed, and stay inspired. Embrace creativity, innovation, and continuous learning. Keep your customers at the heart of everything you do and never stop striving for excellence. The digital marketing world is full of opportunities, and with the right approach, you can achieve remarkable success for your franchise or business.

Thank you for joining me on this journey. I wish you continued growth, success, and fulfilment in all your digital marketing endeavours.

Appendix A: Glossary of Key Terms

Digital marketing involves a wide range of concepts, tools, and strategies. To help you navigate this complex landscape, here's a glossary of key terms that you'll encounter throughout your digital marketing journey.

A/B Testing

A method of comparing two versions of a webpage, email, or ad to see which performs better. Also known as split testing, it helps determine the most effective elements for a campaign.

Analytics

The data and metrics used to measure the performance of digital marketing campaigns. Tools like Google Analytics provide insights into website traffic, user behaviour, and conversions.

B2B (Business-to-Business)

A type of transaction or marketing strategy where businesses sell products or services to other businesses.

B2C (Business-to-Consumer)

A type of transaction or marketing strategy where businesses sell products or services directly to consumers.

Bounce Rate

The percentage of visitors who navigate away from a website after viewing only one page. A high bounce rate may indicate that the website content is not engaging or relevant.

Call-to-Action (CTA)

A prompt that encourages users to take a specific action, such as "Buy Now," "Sign Up," or "Learn More." CTAs are crucial for guiding users toward conversions.

Click-Through Rate (CTR)

The percentage of users who click on a link, ad, or CTA after seeing it. CTR is a key metric for measuring the effectiveness of digital marketing campaigns.

Content Marketing

A strategy focused on creating and distributing valuable, relevant content to attract and engage a target audience. Content marketing can include blogs, videos, infographics, and more.

Conversion Rate

The percentage of users who complete a desired action, such as making a purchase, filling out a form, or signing up for a newsletter. High conversion rates indicate effective marketing efforts.

Cost Per Click (CPC)

The amount paid for each click on a paid advertisement. CPC is commonly used in pay-per-click (PPC) advertising models like Google Ads.

Customer Acquisition Cost (CAC)

The total cost of acquiring a new customer, including marketing and sales expenses. Lowering CAC while maintaining or increasing sales is a key goal for marketers.

Customer Lifetime Value (CLV)

The total revenue that a customer is expected to generate for a business over the course of their relationship. Increasing CLV is a sign of successful customer retention strategies.

Display Ads

Banner ads that appear on websites, apps, or social media platforms. Display ads can include images, text, and interactive elements.

Engagement Rate

A metric that measures the level of interaction users have with content, such as likes, shares, comments, and clicks. High engagement rates indicate that content is resonating with the audience.

Impression

The number of times an ad or piece of content is shown to users. Impressions are often used to measure the reach of a campaign.

Influencer Marketing

A strategy that involves partnering with influencers—individuals with a large online following—to promote a product or service. Influencer marketing leverages the trust and authority influencers have with their audience.

Keyword

A word or phrase that users enter into search engines when looking for information. Keywords are the foundation of SEO and PPC campaigns.

Landing Page

A standalone webpage designed to capture leads or drive conversions. Landing pages are often used in conjunction with digital ads or email campaigns.

Lookalike Audience

An audience that shares similar characteristics with an existing customer base. Lookalike audiences are used in digital advertising to find new potential customers.

Organic Traffic

Visitors who come to a website through unpaid search results. Organic traffic is driven by SEO efforts rather than paid advertising.

Pay-Per-Click (PPC)

An online advertising model where advertisers pay a fee each time their ad is clicked. Google Ads is one of the most popular PPC platforms.

Quality Score

A metric used by Google Ads to determine the relevance and quality of an ad. Higher Quality Scores can lead to better ad positions and lower CPC.

Retargeting

A digital marketing strategy that targets users who have previously visited a website or engaged with content. Retargeting ads remind users of a product or service they showed interest in.

Return on Ad Spend (ROAS)

A metric that measures the revenue generated from an ad campaign compared to the cost of the campaign. A higher ROAS indicates a more profitable campaign.

Search Engine Optimisation (SEO)

The process of optimising a website to rank higher in search engine results pages (SERPs) for specific keywords. SEO involves both on-page and off-page tactics.

Social Proof

The concept that people are influenced by the actions and opinions of others. Social proof can include customer reviews, testimonials, and user-generated content.

Target Audience

The specific group of people that a marketing campaign is aimed at. A well-defined target audience is crucial for the success of any marketing effort.

Appendix B: Additional Resources and Further Reading

To continue your digital marketing education and stay ahead of the curve, here are some additional resources and recommended reading materials:

Online Courses and Certifications

- **Google Digital Garage:** Offers free courses on a wide range of digital marketing topics, including SEO, SEM, and analytics. Google Digital Garage
- **Facebook Blueprint:** Provides free training on Facebook and Instagram advertising, with the option to earn certifications. Facebook Blueprint
- **HubSpot Academy:** Offers free online courses in inbound marketing, content marketing, and social media. HubSpot Academy
- **Moz Academy:** Provides paid courses on SEO, link building, and local search marketing. Moz Academy

Books

- **"Contagious: How to Build Word of Mouth in the Digital Age" by Jonah Berger:** A must-read for understanding why some ideas go viral and how you can apply those principles to your marketing efforts.
- **"Jab, Jab, Jab, Right Hook: How to Tell Your Story in a Noisy Social World" by Gary Vaynerchuk:** A guide to creating compelling content tailored for each social media platform.
- **"Made to Stick: Why Some Ideas Survive and Others Die" by Chip Heath and Dan Heath:** Offers insights into what makes ideas memorable and how you can apply those lessons to your marketing.

- **"Killing Marketing: How Innovative Businesses Are Turning Marketing Cost into Profit" by Joe Pulizzi and Robert Rose:** Explores the changing role of marketing in modern businesses and how you can turn it into a profit centre.

Blogs and Websites

- **Moz Blog:** Offers insights on SEO, link building, and search engine marketing. Moz Blog
- **HubSpot Blog:** Covers a wide range of digital marketing topics, from content marketing to social media strategy. HubSpot Blog
- **Search Engine Journal:** Provides the latest news and insights on SEO, PPC, and content marketing. Search Engine Journal
- **Social Media Examiner:** Offers tips and strategies for effective social media marketing. Social Media Examiner

Tools

- **Google Analytics:** Essential for tracking website traffic, user behaviour, and conversions. Google Analytics
- **Canva:** A user-friendly design tool for creating professional-quality graphics for your marketing campaigns. Canva
- **Hootsuite:** A social media management tool that allows you to schedule posts, track engagement, and manage multiple accounts. Hootsuite
- **SEMrush:** A powerful tool for SEO, keyword research, and competitive analysis. SEMrush

Appendix C: Templates and Checklists for Your Marketing Efforts

To help you implement the strategies discussed in this book, here are some practical templates and checklists that you can use in your digital marketing efforts.

1. Digital Marketing Strategy Template

Goal Setting:

- Define your overall business goals.
- Set specific, measurable, achievable, relevant, and time-bound (SMART) marketing objectives.

Audience Research:

- Identify your target audience demographics.
- Research audience interests, behaviours, and pain points.
- Create buyer personas.

Platform Selection:

- Choose the digital marketing platforms that align with your objectives and audience.
  - Google Ads
  - Facebook Ads
  - Instagram Ads
  - Google Business Profiles

Content and Messaging:

- Develop a content calendar.
- Define key messages and themes.

- Align content with the customer journey stages (awareness, consideration, decision).

Budgeting and Resource Allocation:

- Set your digital marketing budget.
- Allocate resources for content creation, ad spend, and tools.

Measurement and KPIs:

- Identify key performance indicators (KPIs) such as ROI, CTR, and conversion rate.
- Set up tracking and reporting tools (Google Analytics, Facebook Ads Manager).

2. Social Media Content Calendar Template

Date	Platform	Content Type	Topic/Theme	CTA	Notes
01/10/2024	Facebook	Post	Product Launch	Learn More	Link to landing page
03/10/2024	Instagram	Story	Behind-the-Scenes	Swipe Up	Behind-the-scenes of product prep
05/10/2024	LinkedIn	Article	Industry Trends	Read More	Link to blog post
07/10/2024	Twitter	Tweet	Customer Testimonial	Visit Website	Quote from a satisfied

Date	Platform	Content Type	Topic/Theme	CTA	Notes
10/10/2024	Facebook	Live Video	Q&A Session	Join Us	customer Live Q&A with product experts

3. Google Ads Campaign Checklist

- **Campaign Objective:**
  - o Define your campaign objective (e.g., traffic, conversions, brand awareness).
- **Keyword Research:**
  - o Use tools like Google Keyword Planner to identify relevant keywords.
  - o Group keywords into ad groups based on themes.
- **Ad Copy:**
  - o Write compelling headlines and descriptions.
  - o Include a strong call-to-action (CTA).
- **Landing Page:**
  - o Ensure the landing page is relevant to the ad.
  - o Optimise for mobile and load speed.
  - o Include a clear CTA on the landing page.
- **Budget and Bidding:**
  - o Set a daily or lifetime budget.
  - o Choose your bidding strategy (e.g., manual CPC, target CPA).
- **Ad Extensions:**
  - o Add relevant ad extensions (e.g., site links, call extensions, location extensions).
- **Tracking and Analytics:**

- o Set up conversion tracking with Google Analytics.
- o Monitor Quality Score and make adjustments as needed.

4. SEO Checklist

- **On-Page SEO:**
  - o Optimise title tags and meta descriptions.
  - o Use header tags (H1, H2, etc.) to structure content.
  - o Include target keywords naturally within the content.
  - o Optimise images with alt text.
- **Technical SEO:**
  - o Ensure your website is mobile-friendly.
  - o Improve site load speed.
  - o Set up an XML sitemap and submit it to Google Search Console.
  - o Use HTTPS for a secure website.
- **Content Strategy:**
  - o Create high-quality, relevant content that addresses your audience's needs.
  - o Update and repurpose older content.
  - o Use internal linking to guide users through your site.
- **Off-Page SEO:**
  - o Build high-quality backlinks from reputable sites.
  - o Engage in guest blogging and influencer partnerships.
  - o Monitor your backlink profile for any toxic links.